# Bulls, Owls, Lambs and Tigers®: Pers

Copyright©2021 Charles J. Clarke III

All rights reserved by accordance with the U.S. copyright act of 1976. The scanning, uploading and electronic sharing, or any other sharing, of any part of this book without the permission of the author constitutes unlawful piracy and theft of the author's intellectual property. If you would like to use <u>any portion</u> (no matter how small) from the book, prior written permission must be obtained by directly contacting the author and receiving written permission to do so.

**No part of this to be used or reproduced in any manner whatsoever without written permission from the author including blogs or anything online.**

> **It is not enough to just mention the author's name and then go on for more than a paragraph about the copyrighted material. (Do not plagiarize. It is unlawful.)**

**Thank you for your support of the author's rights.**

**Library of Congress control number pending.**

**ISBN**

> Bulls, Owls, Lambs and Tigers® is a Registered Federal Trademark of Charles J. Clarke III since 1988.
>
> BOLT™ and Personality Selling™ are trademarks of Charles J. Clarke III.

*Disclaimer: This publication is designed to provide accurate and authoritative information regarding the subject matter covered. It is sold with the understanding that the author is not engaged in rendering legal, accounting, or other professional services. If legal advice or other expert assistance is required, the services of a competent professional person should be sought.*

*-From a Declaration of Principles jointly adopted by a Committee of the American Bar Association and Committee of Publishers and Accountants.* Printed in the United States by CreateSpace, a division of Amazon.com. Available through Amazon and Kindle.

**Bulls, Owls, Lambs and Tigers®: Personality Selling™**

"Bulls, Owls, Lambs, and Tigers®: Personality Selling™" is an "accompanying" book to, "Bulls, Owls, Lambs, and Tigers®." You really need to read both books but if you start with this one, you will understand all the 36 principles in this book. Then read, "Bulls, Owls, Lambs, and Tigers®."

> **THE PURPOSE OF THIS BOOK IS TO GET YOU TO THINK DIFFERENTLY ABOUT THE SALES PROCESS**

This book is written in Tiger and Bull print with boxes emphasizing important points. Both Bulls and Tigers (1/2 of the population) have told us they appreciate this, because neither of them reads books word for word, as Owls and Lambs do.

Owls and Lambs, I realize I have not defined my terms of Bulls, Owls, Lambs, and Tigers®, yet, but I will.

So, Owls and Lambs bear with us on this one. It is great information.

### 36 Myths in Selling

**MYTHS** What happens with "Myths" in an Industry is they get perpetuated from one book to the next, from one speaker at a convention to the next and on and on. "Salespeople sell the way other salespeople sell" (CCIII) and "Mediocrity" gets passed on.

This book is an attempt to get all of us to "challenge and to continue to challenge," our Belief Systems in each of our Industries, in Sales, and break through Myths that have held us back.

---

Copyright©2021 Charles J. Clarke III. "Bulls, Owls, Lambs and Tigers®" is a registered federal trademark of Charles J. Clarke III since 1988. Personality Selling™ and BOLT™ are Trademarks of Charles J. Clarke III. NO reproduction in any form is allowed.

# Bulls, Owls, Lambs and Tigers®: Personality Selling™

## Table of Contents

| CHAPTER | MYTH | CONTENT | PAGE |
|---|---|---|---|
| 1 |  | BULLS, OWLS, LAMBS AND TIGERS® | 1 |
| 2 |  | QUIZ TO TEST YOUR BELIEF SYSTEM | 11 |
| 3 |  | TORTURING OUR BUYERS | 17 |
| 4 | 1 | EARNING THE RIGHT TO CLOSE | 22 |
| 5 | 2 | SOCIAL FIRST | 26 |
| 6 | 3 | SELLING THE COMPANY'S VISION | 29 |
| 7 | 4 | DEMONSTRATION AS THE MOST IMPORTANT VARIABLE | 32 |
| 8 | 5 | ASKING FOR THE SALE 100% OF THE TIME | 37 |
| 9 | 6 | GETTING THE CHECK THE FIRST DAY | 47 |
| 10 | 7 | BUYING WITHOUT THE SPOUSE BEING THERE | 53 |
| 11 | 8 | CROSSED ARMS AND NO SMILE | 56 |
| 12 | 9 | CONTROLLING THE SALE | 59 |
| 13 | 10 | STATING, RESTATING AND VERIFYING WHAT THE BUYER JUST SAID | 64 |
| 14 | 11 | AVOIDING TALKING ABOUT THE PRICE RIGHT AWAY | 67 |
| 15 | 12 | WOMEN MAKING THE DECISION OF BUYING | 71 |
| 16 | 13 | CREATING URGENCY | 74 |
| 17 | 14 | MEN BEING MORE LOGICAL & WOMEN BEING MORE EMOTIONAL | 81 |
| 18 | 15 | KITCHEN AND MASTER BATHROOM AS THE MOST IMPORTANT ROOMS IN A HOME | 83 |
| 19 | 16 | FINDING COMMON GROUND | 89 |
| 20 | 17 | MEMORIZING SCRIPTS | 92 |
| 21 | 18 | CLOSING RATIOS (1 IN 10) | 97 |
| 22 | 19 | NEGOTIATING | 102 |
| 23 | 20 | FOLLOW UP AND GETTING THEM TO COME BACK | 111 |

# Bulls, Owls, Lambs and Tigers®: Personality Selling™

## Table of Contents

### (CONTINUED)

| CHAPTER | MYTH | CONTENT | PAGE |
|---|---|---|---|
| 24 | 21 | HAVING BEEN TO YOUR WEBSITE | 113 |
| 25 | 22 | BUYING ON EMOTION AND JUSTIFYING WITH LOGIC | 115 |
| 26 | 23 | SELLING TO THE 50+ (SENIOR BUYER) | 118 |
| 27 | 24 | SELLING GOLF COURSE COMMUNITIES AND RESORT COMMUNITIES | 121 |
| 28 | 25 | 100+ OBJECTIONS | 124 |
| 29 | 26 | SELLING "HIGH-END" PROPERTIES | 131 |
| 30 | 27 | ASKING QUESTIONS STANDING UP | 134 |
| 31 | 28 | BRINGING OUT THE PAPERWORK (CONTRACT) AFTER THEY ALREADY SAID "NO" | 141 |
| 32 | 29 | SELLING AUTOMOBILES AND VANS AND GETTING THEM TO DRIVE THEM FIRST | 148 |
| 33 | 30 | SELLING AT SHOWS & CONVENTIONS | 155 |
| 34 | 31 | SELLING RETAIL (SUIT EXAMPLE) | 158 |
| 35 | 32 | LOOKING FOR BUYING SIGNS | 163 |
| 36 | 33 | SELLING INTANGABLES | 166 |
| 37 | 34 | RESTAURANT INDUSTRY & CUSTOMER SERVICE INDUSTRY | 171 |
| 38 | 35 | MARITAL RELATIONSHIPS | 175 |
| 39 | 36 | SELLING FLAWED PRODUCT & DESIGN | 181 |
| 40 | | CONCLUSION | 183 |
| 41 | | FINAL THOUGHTS | 187 |

**Bulls, Owls, Lambs and Tigers®: Personality Selling™**

# CHAPTER 1

*Portions of this chapter are excerpts from Charles J. Clarke III's, "Bulls, Owls, Lambs and Tigers®."*

## BULLS, OWLS, LAMBS AND TIGERS®

**READ EACH DESCRIPTION AND THEN RANK IN ORDER WHICH ONE IS MOST LIKELY YOU (2$^{ND}$, 3$^{RD}$, AND 4$^{TH}$). ACTUALLY, WRITE IT DOWN.**

### THE BULL (CONTROL) #_____

- BOTTOM LINE, GET TO THE POINT
- CAN BE SOMEWHAT ABRASIVE PERSONALITY

### THE OWL (ORDER) #_____

- EXTREMELY ANALYTICAL, DETAIL ORIENTED
- PERSON WHO WANTS TO CORRECT EVERYTHING YOU DO

### THE LAMB (PLEASING OTHERS) #_____

- PERSON WHO WANTS TO PLEASE EVERYBODY
- TAKES A LONG TIME TO MAKE UP THEIR MIND

### THE TIGER (FUN AND EXCITEMENT) #_____

- FUN AND EXCITING TYPE OF PERSON
- DISTRACTED BY SHINY OBJECTS, WITH LOW ATTENTION SPAN

I AM A _____ WITH _____.

    #1 ANSWER                  #2 ANSWER

© 2021 Charles J. Clarke III. "Bulls, Owls, Lambs and Tigers®" is a registered federal trademark of Charles J. Clarke III since 1988. Personality Selling™ and BOLT™ are Trademarks of Charles J. Clarke III. NO reproduction in any form is allowed.

# BULLS, OWLS, LAMBS AND TIGERS® IS NOT GENDER-BASED

HALF THE BULLS ARE WOMEN AND HALF THE LAMBS ARE MEN. IT IS NOT GENDER BASED.

## YES, I DO KNOW MY BIOLOGY, BUT IN MY ANIMAL PERSONALITY SYSTEM, ½ THE BULLS ARE WOMEN

"IF A SALESPERSON ALWAYS SELLS THE WAY THEY WOULD LIKE TO BE SOLD, THEY COULD BE LOSING APPROXIMATELY ½ TO ¾'S OF THEIR POTENTIAL SALES."

CHARLES J. CLARKE III

"IF A MARKETING PERSON ALWAYS MARKETS THE WAY THEY WOULD LIKE TO BE MARKETED, THEY WILL **NOT** BE REACHING ABOUT ½ TO ¾'S OF THEIR POTENTIAL MARKET."

CHARLES J. CLARKE III

© 2021 Charles J. Clarke III. "Bulls, Owls, Lambs and Tigers®" is a registered federal trademark of Charles J. Clarke III since 1988. Personality Selling™ and BOLT™ are Trademarks of Charles J. Clarke III. NO reproduction in any form is allowed.

**Bulls, Owls, Lambs and Tigers®: Personality Selling™**

> # "IF A DESIGNER ALWAYS DESIGNS WHAT THEY LIKE AND PUTS IN ONLY THE FEATURES <u>THEY</u> LIKE, THEY WILL PROBABLY NOT BE REACHING ½ TO ¾ OF THEIR POTENTIAL CUSTOMERS."
>
> **CHARLES J. CLARKE III**

THIS APPLIES TO <u>EVERY</u> ASPECT OF SELLING.

LET'S GO BACK TO YOUR ANSWERS ON WHAT YOU THINK YOUR ANIMAL PERSONALITY IS.

AN ANSWER I GET FROM SOME PEOPLE IN MY SEMINARS IS, "WELL I THINK I HAVE ALL FOUR OF THESE CHARACTERISTICS IN ME." WHAT A "COP OUT!" (THAT'S A BULL PHRASE.)

OF COURSE, WE ALL HAVE ALL FOUR OF THESE ANIMALS IN US, BUT EVERYONE HAS ONE THAT IS THE MOST "DOMINANT" AND ONE THAT IS THE LEAST "DOMINANT."

"OK," SOME PEOPLE ARE "CLOSE" ON SOME OF THEM, BUT YOU KNOW WHICH ONE IS MOST LIKE YOU AND LEAST LIKE YOU.

ACTUALLY, IN THIS "FIRST PASS AT JUDGING OUR OWN PERSONALITY, ABOUT HALF THE PEOPLE REALLY DO NOT SEE THEMSELVES AS THEY REALLY ARE."

DO PEOPLE CHANGE? CAN THEY CHANGE THEIR PERSONALITY? MY ANSWER IS THEY CAN "MODIFY" AND "ADAPT," BUT NOT REALLY CHANGE.

WHAT DO YOU THINK?

THIS IS JUST A THUMB NAIL SKETCH OF EACH ANIMAL. AGAIN, PLEASE REFER TO MY FULL VOLUME BOOK, "BULLS, OWLS, LAMBS & TIGERS®."

OTHER IDEAS FROM OUR RESEARCH ON EACH ANIMAL PERSONALITY, IS THAT:

BULLS AND TIGERS (APPROXIMATELY 50% OF THE POPULATION WHEN COMBINED) SAY THEY:

1) <u>HAVE</u> BOUGHT THE FIRST DAY,
2) <u>WOULD</u> BUY THE FIRST DAY IF THEY WERE <u>READY, WILLING AND ABLE,</u> AND
3) SAY THEY WOULD <u>PREFER</u> TO BUY THE FIRST DAY. (THIS IS ON HOMES, YACHTS OR ANY HIGH-END PRODUCT.)

## Bulls, Owls, Lambs and Tigers®: Personality Selling™

IF YOU ARE AN OWL OR LAMB, YOU DO **NOT** BELIEVE THAT LAST STATEMENT. WHY? BECAUSE **YOU** WOULD NOT DO THAT **YOURSELF!**

OUR #1 OBJECTION IS OUR OWN!

**WE JUDGE OTHER PEOPLE OUT OF OUR OWN PERSONALITY AND BEHAVIOR AND THUS LOSE POTENTIAL SALES.**

YOUR THOUGHTS?

# Bulls, Owls, Lambs and Tigers®: Personality Selling™

**BRIEF SUMMARY OF MY FOUR ANIMALS**

# THE BULL

## CONTROL-ORIENTED

- LIKES THE BOTTOM LINE – "GET TO THE POINT" (NOT A TO Z, JUST Z), (THEY ASK ABOUT PRICE RIGHT AWAY)
- FAST TO DECIDE (THEY SAY THEY HAVE BOUGHT THE FIRST DAY AND WOULD PREFER TO BUY THE FIRST DAY)
- FAST-PACED
- YOU BUILD RAPPORT WITH THEM BY **NOT** EMPHAZING SOCIAL FIRST
- RESULTS-ORIENTED
- NEEDS TO CONTROL SITUATION
- PRESTIGE AND STATUS ARE MORE IMPORTANT THAN SECURITY
- LIKES CHALLENGES
- LIKES FREEDOM FROM CONTROL
- BUSINESS FIRST, THEN POSSIBLE SOCIAL (THEY WANT COMMERCE FIRST)
- LOVES TO NEGOTIATE – (THEY BUY WHEN THEY BELIEVE NO ONE ELSE WILL GET A BETTER PRICE.) YOU DO NOT HAVE TO LOWER THE PRICE WITH THEM. THEY JUST NEED TO KNOW NO ONE IS GOING TO GET A BETTER PRICE.

### FOLLOW-UP FOR THE BULL

- GIVE THEM A REASON TO BUY NOW. (URGENCY CLOSES WORK WELL WITH BULLS) THEY ARE CAPABLE OF FAST DECISION MAKING.
- ALWAYS HAVE SOMETHING FOR THEM WHEN YOU PHONE OR WRITE. BULLS DO NOT WANT A SOCIAL CALL AND THEY WILL EXPECT YOU TO GET TO THE POINT OR THE REASON FOR THE CALL.
- ADDRESS BUSINESS FIRST, AND THEN SOCIAL (POSSIBLY) NEXT.
- FIRST EXPLAIN HOW YOUR PRODUCT WILL HELP (OR AFFECT) THEM. EVEN A BULL WITH LAMB TENDENCIES WANTS TO KNOW THE "ME" RESULTS FIRST, AND THEN HOW IT WILL AFFECT OTHERS.
- LOVES TO NEGOTIATE AND HAS TO FEEL THAT THEY RECEIVED A "ONE OF A KIND" PRODUCT, PRICE OR "DEAL." THEY BUY BECAUSE THEY LIKE IT, NOT BECAUSE YOU BUILD VALUE.
- MAKE SURE FREQUENCY OF FOLLOW-UP (AND THE CONTENT) IS LIMITED. STATE YOUR PURPOSE FOR WRITING OR CALLING, IN YOUR FIRST REMARKS. SINCE BULLS WILL BUY THE FIRST DAY, FOLLOW-UP IS USUALLY AFTER THE SALE.

© 2021 Charles J. Clarke III. "Bulls, Owls, Lambs and Tigers®" is a registered federal trademark of Charles J. Clarke III since 1988. Personality Selling™ and BOLT™ are Trademarks of Charles J. Clarke III. NO reproduction in any form is allowed.

**Bulls, Owls, Lambs and Tigers®: Personality Selling™**

# THE OWL

## ORDER/SYSTEMS AND DETAIL

- LIKES DETAIL AND FULL PRESENTATION FROM A TO Z. (THEY ASK MORE QUESTIONS THAN ANY OF THE OTHER ANIMALS.) LIKES A THROUGH Z, IN ORDER.
- TAKES TIME TO DECIDE AND IS SLOW-PACED
- VERY TIME-CONSCIOUS AND EARLY FOR APPOINTMENTS
- NO MISTAKES (YOURS OR THEIRS)
- DOES NOT LIKE OVER-EXCITEMENT AND EMOTIONALISM
- SECURITY MORE IMPORTANT THAN PRESTIGE AND STATUS
- LIKES BEING ALONE (SOLITUDE)
- BUSINESS FIRST, THEN SOCIAL ("THEY REALLY DON'T WANT TO DRINK YOUR COFFEE.")
- THEY "BUY" WHEN ALL THEIR QUESTIONS HAVE BEEN ANSWERED, AND THEY HAVE **LOTS** OF QUESTIONS

### FOLLOW-UP FOR THE OWL

- AFTER A VERY DETAILED PRESENTATION FROM "A TO Z," AN OWL CAN BE SOLD ON THE SPOT IF THEY HAVE BEEN LOOKING FOR SOME TIME. IF THERE ARE ANY DETAILS MISSING, THEY WILL NEED TO BE ADDRESSED, SYSTEMATICALLY, IN YOUR FOLLOW-UP. ALSO NOTE THAT OWLS HAVE ALREADY VISITED YOU ON THE WEBSITE.
- BE ON TIME, REMEMBERING THAT AN OWL WILL BE <u>EARLY</u> FOR FOLLOW-UP APPOINTMENTS.
- STICK TO BUSINESS AND COVER ANY MISTAKES.
- MAKE DOUBLY SURE THAT YOU "DOT YOUR I'S AND CROSS YOUR T'S."
- KEEP THINGS NON-EMOTIONAL. EXPLORE THE PRACTICAL REASONS TO BUY THE PRODUCT.
- OWLS BUY WITH LOGIC AND JUSTIFY WITH LOGIC (THEY DO NOT BUY ON EMOTION.)
- THEY DO NOT LIKE URGENCY CLOSES OR TAKE-AWAY CLOSES. THEY RESPOND NEGATIVELY TO BOTH.

© 2021 Charles J. Clarke III. "Bulls, Owls, Lambs and Tigers®" is a registered federal trademark of Charles J. Clarke III since 1988. Personality Selling™ and BOLT™ are Trademarks of Charles J. Clarke III. NO reproduction in any form is allowed.

**Bulls, Owls, Lambs and Tigers®: Personality Selling™**

# THE LAMB

## PLEASERS/DON'T LIKE CONFLICT

- LIKES FOR YOU TO BE THEIR FRIEND, GIVE DIRECTION, AND SHOW SUPPORT
- SLOW TO DECIDE AND OFTEN CHANGE THEIR MINDS (HIGH BUYER'S REMORSE)
- UNDERSTANDS YOUR MISTAKES AND FEELS BAD ABOUT THEIR MISTAKES
- VERY EMOTIONAL
- SECURITY IS MORE IMPORTANT THAN PRESTIGE AND STATUS
- AVOIDS CONFLICT
- WANTS PROTECTION AND PEACE
- SOCIAL FIRST THEN BUSINESS; NEEDS TO BUILD RAPPORT FIRST

### FOLLOW-UP FOR THE LAMB

- ABOVE ALL, BE THEIR FRIEND, GIVE DIRECTION AND SHOW SUPPORT.
- LAMBS ARE VERY CONCERNED ABOUT HOW THEIR PURCHASE WILL AFFECT OTHERS.
- TALK EMOTIONALLY ABOUT HOW MUCH THEIR FAMILY AND FRIENDS WILL ENJOY WHATEVER THEY BOUGHT.
- REASSURE THEM OVER AND OVER AGAIN ABOUT WARRANTY AND "ON-SITE SERVICE DEPARTMENT, SHOULD ANYTHING GO WRONG."
- SECURITY OF THE PURCHASE IS EXTREMELY IMPORTANT TO THEM.
- REASSURE THEM THAT THERE HAVE BEEN MANY SATISFIED CUSTOMERS BEFORE THEM, NOT JUST OF THIS COMPANY, BUT ALSO OF THIS PRODUCT. (TESTIMONIALS ARE VERY IMPORTANT TO THE LAMB.)
- AVOID PRESSURE SALES. INSTEAD, BE THEIR FRIEND; DIRECT THEM TOWARD A DECISION, AND HELP THEM MAKE THAT DECISION. EVENTUALLY, <u>TELL</u> THEM TO BUY -- IN A SOFT WAY.
- THEY DO NOT LIKE URGENCY CLOSES AND, IN FACT, RESPOND NEGATIVELY TO "URGENCY CLOSES" OR "TAKE AWAY CLOSES."

**Bulls, Owls, Lambs and Tigers®: Personality Selling™**

# THE TIGER

## FUN AND EXCITEMENT

- NOT INTO DETAILS – PREFERS OTHERS TO TAKE CARE OF THE DETAILS
- FAST TO DECIDE AND WILL BUY THE FIRST DAY
- FAST-PACED AND IS OFTEN LATE FOR APPOINTMENTS
- LOVES RECOGNITION AND EMOTION. LIKES EXCITEMENT
- PRESTIGE AND STATUS ARE MORE IMPORTANT THAN SECURITY
- LIKES A CHALLENGE
- SOCIAL RELATIONSHIPS ARE IMPORTANT
- SOCIAL FIRST, THEN BUSINESS

**FOLLOW-UP FOR THE TIGER**

- A TIGER WANTS SOCIAL, THEN BUSINESS. AFTER YOUR FIRST ENCOUNTER, MAKE NOTES ABOUT THE TIGER'S FAVORITE TEAMS, ACTIVITIES, AND VACATIONS THEY HAVE PLANNED, AND REFER TO ANY FUN CURRENT NEWS, AFTER YOU HAVE SOLD THEM THE FIRST VISIT. IF HE OR SHE IS A TIGER WITH LAMB TENDENCIES, ASK ABOUT THEIR FAMILY.
- THEY ARE FAST DECISION-MAKERS AND BUY WHEN THEY ARE EXCITED ABOUT THE PRODUCT.
- GET THEM EXCITED AND CLOSE THE SALE THE FIRST DAY.
- THE ATTENTION SPAN OF A TIGER IS SHORT.
- IF YOU DON'T CLOSE TIGERS THE FIRST DAY, YOU PROBABLY WON'T SEE THEM AGAIN.
- TIGERS ENJOY THE LIMELIGHT AND RECOGNITION. REMIND THEM HOW GREAT THEIR FRIENDS WILL THINK THEY ARE, BECAUSE OF THEIR NEW PRODUCT.
- KEEP THE FOLLOW-UP EXCITING, TO THE POINT, VISUAL, SOCIAL FIRST, NOT MUCH DETAIL, VARIED AND TAILOR-MADE

© 2021 Charles J. Clarke III. "Bulls, Owls, Lambs and Tigers®" is a registered federal trademark of Charles J. Clarke III since 1988. Personality Selling™ and BOLT™ are Trademarks of Charles J. Clarke III. NO reproduction in any form is allowed.

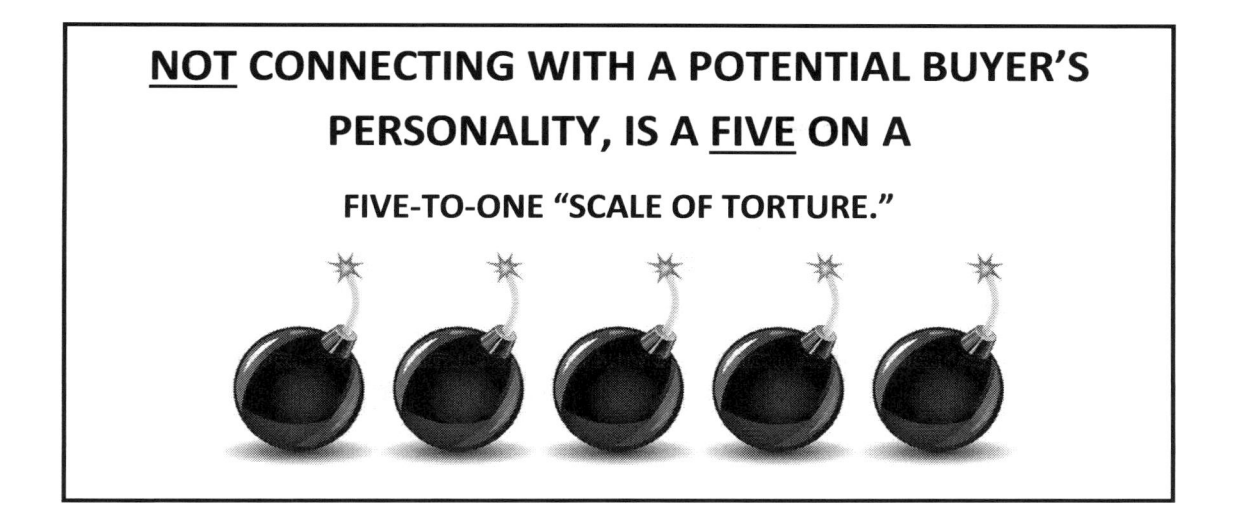

# Bulls, Owls, Lambs and Tigers®: Personality Selling™

**NOT CONNECTING WITH A POTENTIAL BUYER'S PERSONALITY, IS A FIVE ON A**

**FIVE-TO-ONE "SCALE OF TORTURE."**

THIS IS NOT MANIPULATIVE OR PHONEY. YOU REALLY "BECOME" THE OTHER PERSON. START "THINKING" LIKE THE OTHER PERSON OR AT LEAST TRY TO.

**WHEN YOU ARE SELLING TO A BULL, YOU WANT TO "BECOME" THE BULL! WHEN YOU ARE SELLING TO AN OWL, YOU WANT TO "BECOME" THE OWL! WHEN YOU ARE SELLING TO A LAMB, YOU WANT TO "BECOME" THE LAMB! WHEN YOU ARE SELLING TO THE TIGER, YOU WANT TO "BECOME" THE TIGER!**

BOLT™ IS AN ACRONYM FOR BULLS, OWLS, LAMBS AND TIGERS®. THEY ARE BOTH INTERCHANGEABLE.

© 2021 Charles J. Clarke III. "Bulls, Owls, Lambs and Tigers®" is a registered federal trademark of Charles J. Clarke III since 1988. Personality Selling™ and BOLT™ are Trademarks of Charles J. Clarke III. NO reproduction in any form is allowed.

# NOTES

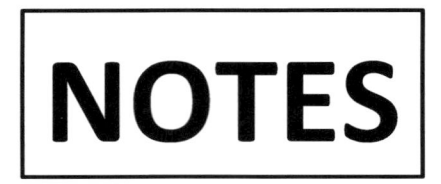

THINGS I AGREE WITH

THINGS I DISAGREE WITH

THINGS I NEED TO WORK ON

ACTION PLAN FOR ME

# CHAPTER 2

## QUESTIONS

*HELLO!*

*BEFORE I BEGIN WITH GIVING YOU MY "OPINION" IN SELLING, LET ME ASK YOU, **YOUR** OPINION.*

*PLEASE GO AHEAD AND ANSWER THESE 36 QUESTIONS BEFORE READING AHEAD.*

*I'M ASKING YOU TO ACTUALLY WRITE IN YOUR BOOK SO YOU CAN REFER BACK TO YOUR ANSWERS LATER.*

*IF YOU ARE A MEGA "OWL" (VERY ANALYTICAL, NEAT AND SYSTEMS- ORIENTED) USE A PENCIL OR AT LEAST RECORD YOUR ANSWERS, SOMEWHERE, FOR FUTURE REFERENCE. OWLS HAVE A HIGHER PREFERENCE FOR **NOT** WRITING IN THEIR BOOKS. LIBRARIANS TAUGHT THEM THAT AND THEY OBEYED. LAMBS (RULES ORIENTED INDIVIDUALS) ALSO PREFER NOT TO WRITE IN THEIR BOOKS.*

*YOU WILL GET SO MUCH MORE OUT OF THIS BOOK IF YOU REALLY DO READ ALL THE QUESTIONS AND <u>WRITE</u> DOWN ALL YOUR ANSWERS! (BULLS, GO AHEAD AND DO IT!)*

*OF COURSE, SOME OF THESE QUESTIONS HAVE TO DO WITH THE <u>TYPE</u> OF PRODUCT YOU ARE SELLING.*

*THANK YOU,*

*CHARLES J. CLARKE III*

*P.S. IF YOU HAVEN'T READ MY "BULLS, OWLS, LAMBS & TIGERS®," YOU NEED TO GET IT AND READ IT! HOWEVER, THIS BOOK STANDS ON ITS OWN!*

# Bulls, Owls, Lambs and Tigers®: Personality Selling™

## "36 STATEMENTS TO DISCOVER YOUR BELIEF STATEMENT IN SELLING"

*(SOME OF THE EXAMPLES ARE OBVIOUSLY NOT WHAT YOU SELL, BUT RATHER ANSWER YOUR BELIEF SYSTEM.)*

TOTAL UP YOUR TOTAL # OF YES'S AND YOUR TOTAL # OF NO'S OUT OF THESE 36 QUESTIONS.

1) A SALESPERSON HAS TO ALWAYS EARN THE RIGHT TO CLOSE. YES/NO

2) IT IS OF UTMOST IMPORTANCE TO ALWAYS TALK ABOUT SOCIAL FIRST (BUILD RAPPORT) RATHER THAN BUSINESS FIRST (COMMERCE). YES/NO

3) IN SALES IT IS OF UTMOST IMPORTANCE TO SELL THE CONCEPT OF THE "COMPANY'S VISION" AND TELL THE COMPANY'S STORY AT THE BEGINNING, IN THE FIRST FEW MINUTES. YES/NO

4) OF ALL THE STEPS OF THE CRITICAL PATH OF SELLING, THE OUTRIGHT MOST IMPORTANT STEP IS "DEMONSTRATION," IN ORDER TO DIFFERENTIATE YOUR COMPANY FROM OTHER COMPANIES. YES/NO

5) IT WOULD BE TOO PUSHY TO, 100% OF THE TIME, ASK FOR THE SALE. YES/NO

6) IT IS "VERY RARE" FOR SOMEONE TO "BUY" (GIVE A CHECK AND SIGN A CONTRACT), THE FIRST TIME THEY ARE PRESENTED WITH YOUR PRODUCT. YES/NO

7) IF PEOPLE ARE MARRIED, THEY WILL NOT "BUY" IF THEIR SPOUSE IS NOT THERE, IF IT WAS SOMETHING THAT WOULD INVOLVE THE SPOUSE. YES/NO

8) CROSSED ARMS AND NO SMILE MEANS THAT A PERSON IS DEFENSIVE. YES/NO

9) IT IS VERY IMPORTANT THAT THE SALESPERSON TAKES CONTROL AND MAINTAINS CONTROL THROUGHOUT THE SALES PROCESS, AND THAT THE BUYER IS TOTALLY MADE AWARE OF THIS. YES/NO

10) IT IS VERY IMPORTANT TO "ALWAYS STATE, RESTATE AND VERIFY" WHAT THE BUYER JUST SAID. YES/NO

11) IF A BUYER ASKS FOR THE PRICE RIGHT AWAY, THE SALESPERSON SHOULD AVOID TELLING THE BUYER THE PRICE RIGHT AWAY AND STAY ON COURSE. YES/NO

© 2021 Charles J. Clarke III. "Bulls, Owls, Lambs and Tigers®" is a registered federal trademark of Charles J. Clarke III since 1988. Personality Selling™ and BOLT™ are Trademarks of Charles J. Clarke III. NO reproduction in any form is allowed.

# Bulls, Owls, Lambs and Tigers®: Personality Selling™

12) IF A COUPLE IS MARRIED, THE WOMAN ALWAYS MAKES THE FINAL DECISION IN BUYING, IF IT APPLIES TO A HOME OR SOMETHING FOR THE HOME. YES/NO

13) EVEN IF THERE IS NOT AN URGENT SITUATION, THE SALESPERSON NEEDS TO CREATE "URGENCY," IN ORDER TO MOTIVATE THE BUYER. YES/NO

14) MEN ARE ALWAYS MORE "LOGICAL" IN BUYING, WHILE WOMEN ARE ALWAYS MORE "EMOTIONAL." YES/NO

15) THE KITCHEN AND THE MASTER BATHROOM WERE, AND STILL ARE, THE MOST IMPORTANT ROOMS IN A HOME FOR A BUYER. YES/NO

16) IT IS OF UTMOST IMPORTANCE TO FIND "COMMON GROUND" WITH THE BUYER AND MAINTAIN THAT "COMMON GROUND" THROUGHOUT THE SELLING PROCESS. YES/NO

17) MEMORIZING "SCRIPTS," "WORD FOR WORD," AND USING THESE MEMORIZED SCRIPTS VERBATIM IS EXTREMELY IMPORTANT FOR THE SALESPERSON TO BECOME THE ABSOLUTE BEST. YES/NO

18) CALCULATING CLOSING RATIOS IS NOT REALLY ACCURATE FOR OUR BUSINESS. YES/NO

19) IT IS BEST TO ALWAYS PRICE YOUR PRODUCT HIGHER THAN THE PRICE YOU WOULD REALLY SELL IT, SO YOU CAN NEGOTIATE THE PRICE LOWER. YES/NO

20) THE MOST IMPORTANT ACCOMPLISHMENT A SALESPERSON CAN ACCOMPLISH ON THE FIRST VISIT IS TO GIVE THE BEST PRESENTATION POSSIBLE TO GET THE BUYER EXCITED ENOUGH FOR THEM TO COME BACK. YES/NO

21) 92% OF ALL POTENTIAL BUYERS HAVE ALREADY GONE TO YOUR WEBSITE BEFORE VISITING YOU. YES/NO

22) ALL BUYERS BUY WITH EMOTION AND JUSTIFY IT WITH LOGIC. YES/NO

23) IN SELLING TO 50+ BUYERS, THEY REALLY NEED TO BE TREATED DIFFERENTLY AND CERTAINLY WOULD NOT BUY ON THE FIRST DAY. YES/NO

24) SELLING GOLF COURSE COMMUNITIES AND RESORT COMMUNITIES IS VERY DIFFERENT FROM SELLING NON-RESORT COMMUNITIES. YES/NO

© 2021 Charles J. Clarke III. "Bulls, Owls, Lambs and Tigers®" is a registered federal trademark of Charles J. Clarke III since 1988. Personality Selling™ and BOLT™ are Trademarks of Charles J. Clarke III. NO reproduction in any form is allowed.

# Bulls, Owls, Lambs and Tigers®: Personality Selling™

25) THERE COULD BE LITERALLY 100 OBJECTIONS OF WHY A BUYER DOESN'T BUY. YES/NO

26) SELLING "HIGH-END" PRODUCTS REQUIRES A VERY DIFFERENT SKILL SET THAN SELLING "LOWER END" PRODUCT. YES/NO

27) IT IS BEST TO ALWAYS ASK QUALIFYING QUESTIONS (READY, WILLING, & ABLE), STANDING UP WHERE THE BUYER IS RELAXED, RATHER THAN GOING INTO YOUR OFFICE, IN THE FIRST COUPLE OF MINUTES. YES/NO

28) IF THE BUYER IS A READY, WILLING, AND ABLE BUYER, AND SAYS "NO, THEY DO NOT WANT TO GO AHEAD WITH THIS TODAY," IT WOULD BE RUDE AND PUSHY TO BRING OUT THE (CONTRACT) PURCHASE AGREEMENT AND START WRITING ON IT. YES/NO

29) IN SELLING AUTOMOBILES AND VANS, IT IS BEST FOR THE SALESPERSON TO "INSIST" ON THE POTENTIAL BUYER TO DRIVE THE VEHICLE BEFORE PURCHASING. YES/NO

30) IN SELLING AT SHOWS OR CONVENTIONS, THE MOST IMPORTANT THING YOU CAN DO RIGHT AWAY, IS TO TELL A LITTLE ABOUT YOUR COMPANY. YES/NO

31) IN SELLING RETAIL, IF YOU WERE SELLING EXPENSIVE MEN'S SUITS, IT WOULD BE TOO PUSHY TO TRY TO CLOSE A PROSPECT, VERSUS LETTING THEM DECIDE ON THEIR OWN. YES/NO

32) IN SELLING, WE HAVE TO ALWAYS BE LOOKING FOR "BUYING SIGNS," AND ACT UPON THOSE BUYING SIGNS. YES/NO

33) SELLING INTANGIBLES (SOMETHING YOU CAN'T SEE) IS HARDER THAN SELLING TANGIBLES. YES/NO

34) IN A RESTAURANT, A WAITER OR WAITRESS SHOULD ALWAYS TELL THEIR CUSTOMER ABOUT THEIR "SPECIALS" (IF THEY HAVE SPECIALS.) YES/NO

35) SELLING IN A MARRIAGE IS VERY DIFFERENT FROM SELLING PRODUCT. YES/NO

36) MASTER CLOSERS CANNOT OVERCOME BAD OR FLAWED DESIGN AND PRODUCT. YES/NO

### ADD UP YOUR SCORE

TOTAL # OF YES'S_____     TOTAL # OF NO'S_____

PLEASE DO THIS TEST AND TOTAL YOUR ANSWERS BEFORE YOU READ ON!

© 2021 Charles J. Clarke III. "Bulls, Owls, Lambs and Tigers®" is a registered federal trademark of Charles J. Clarke III since 1988. Personality Selling™ and BOLT™ are Trademarks of Charles J. Clarke III. NO reproduction in any form is allowed.

# Bulls, Owls, Lambs and Tigers®: Personality Selling™

WHEN I DO THIS AND WHEN MASTER CLOSERS DO THIS, WE END UP WITH **ZERO** YES'S. THE AVERAGE NUMBER OF YES'S WE FIND ARE ABOUT 50% OR HIGHER AND THERE ARE ALWAYS SOME THAT HAVE ALL YES'S

AGAIN, THERE ARE NOT NECESSARILY RIGHT OR WRONG ANSWERS. IT IS JUST YOUR OPINION. HOWEVER, WOULD YOU AGREE THAT YOUR "OPINIONS" ACTUALLY SHAPE YOUR PERFORMANCE IN SELLING?

> **THE MORE YES'S YOU HAVE THE MORE "BLOCKS" YOU HAVE.**

> **THERE IS A DIRECT CORRELATION BETWEEN "ZERO YES'S" AND BEING A MASTER CLOSER.**

> **THE MORE YES'S YOU HAVE, THE MORE PRONE YOU ARE TO TORTURE YOUR BUYERS.**

> **IF YOU HAD 17 OR MORE YES'S, YOU ARE A REGULAR "TORTURE CHAMBER" TO YOUR BUYERS.**
>
> **YOU CAN CHANGE, IF YOU WANT TO!**

YOUR THOUGHTS?

IF YOU HAVE 36 NO'S AND ZERO YES'S "DEMAND YOUR MONEY BACK," BECAUSE YOU ARE "ALREADY THERE!"

# NOTES

THINGS I AGREE WITH

THINGS I DISAGREE WITH

THINGS I NEED TO WORK ON

ACTION PLAN FOR ME

# Bulls, Owls, Lambs and Tigers®: Personality Selling™

## CHAPTER 3

### TORTURING OUR BUYERS

LET ME ASK YOU A QUESTION:

> HAVE YOU EVER BEEN TORTURED BY A SALESPERSON? HOW MANY TIMES? WHEN WAS THE LAST TIME?

## WE HAVE ALL BEEN TORTURED BY SALESPEOPLE.

## AND

## WE IN SALES ALL HAVE TORTURED BUYERS IN OUR OWN WAY.

BE SURE TO WRITE DOWN IN THE NOTES, AT THE END OF THIS CHAPTER, SOME OF YOUR GREAT EXAMPLES OF HOW YOU HAVE BEEN "TORTURED" BY A SALESPERSON. (I WOULD LOVE YOU TO EMAIL ME SOME OF THESE EXAMPLES.)

> **EXAMPLE 1 OF TORTURING YOUR BUYER**
> TRYING TO BUY A LARGE, FLAT SCREEN, HIGH-DEFINITION TELEVISION AT AN ELECTRONICS STORE:

> THIS HAPPENED WHEN FLAT SCREEN, HIGH-DEFINITION TELEVISIONS HAD JUST COME OUT.

I WANTED TO BUY A VERY LARGE SCREEN TELEVISION FOR MY ENTIRE FAMILY. I WANTED TO BUY THE KIND OF TELEVISION WITH ALL THE ACCESSORIES OF SURROUND SOUND, ETC. I THOUGHT I WOULD BE PAYING AROUND $6,000, BUT I WASN'T SURE. REMEMBER, THAT IS WHEN THEY FIRST CAME OUT.

# Bulls, Owls, Lambs and Tigers®: Personality Selling™

I WOULD LOVE TO SAY THE NAME OF THIS NATION-WIDE ELECTRONICS STORE, THAT I TRULY LOVE, BUT I DON'T WANT TO GET SUED. THEY USUALLY GIVE <u>GREAT</u> SERVICE! MY POINT IS THAT SOMETIMES SALESPEOPLE ARE SO KNOWLEDGEABLE IN ELECTRONIC EQUIPMENT, COMPUTERS, SMART PHONES, ETC., THAT:

**THEY THINK <u>EVERYONE</u> WANTS ALL THEIR KNOWLEDGE. NOT ALL DO!**

TWO NIGHTS BEFORE CHRISTMAS I WALKED IN AND SAID TO THE GREETER AT THE DOOR, "I'M LOOKING FOR A VERY LARGE, FLAT SCREEN TELEVISION WITH HIGH DEFINITION."

HE IMMEDIATELY HAD ME WITH A SALESPERSON WITH WHOM I REPEATED MY QUESTION, ADDING "WHAT DO YOU THINK WOULD BE THE PRICE OF THIS TYPE OF TELEVISION?" HE WALKED ME BACK TO THE TELEVISION DEPARTMENT AND ASKED ME, "HOW FAMILIAR ARE YOU WITH THE FLAT SCREEN, HIGH-DEFINITION TELEVISION, AND HOW IT WORKS?"

MY RESPONSE WAS SOMETHING LIKE, "I REALLY DO NOT KNOW HOW IT WORKS. I JUST WANT TO MAKE SURE I CAN GET IT DELIVERED BY TOMORROW AND THAT IT DOESN'T GO TOO FAR OVER WHAT I HAVE IN MIND, PRICE-WISE."

HE DID NOT ANSWER MY QUESTIONS. INSTEAD, HE SAID, "SINCE YOU ARE NOT TOO FAMILIAR WITH HOW IT WORKS, LET ME BRIEFLY EXPLAIN THAT TO YOU," AND STARTED WHAT TURNED OUT TO BE A 3 MINUTE AND 40 SECOND EXPLANATION. (I KNOW THIS BECAUSE I USUALLY "TIME" PRESENTATIONS - GOOD ONES AND BAD ONES.)

AT THE END OF HIS 3 MINUTE AND 40 SECONDS EXPLANATION, HE ASKED ME IF I HAD ANY QUESTIONS.

NOW YOU MIGHT BE ASKING YOURSELF (IF YOU'RE STILL READING THIS), WHY DID I ALLOW THAT "ABUSE/TORTURE" TO CONTINUE?

IT WAS THE HOLIDAY SEASON AND I WAS IN A GOOD MOOD. I REALLY DIDN'T WANT TO HURT HIS FEELINGS, AND I REALIZED I WAS IN THE MIDDLE OF AN EXPERIMENT. (MINE)

**EXPERIMENT: "HOW MUCH TORTURE CAN A BUYER ACCEPT?"**

THE STORY IS NOT OVER YET.

I POINTED TO A TELEVISION THAT SEEMED TO MEET MY NEEDS AND ASKED THE PRICE OF THE TELEVISION.

© 2021 Charles J. Clarke III. "Bulls, Owls, Lambs and Tigers®" is a registered federal trademark of Charles J. Clarke III since 1988. Personality Selling™ and BOLT™ are Trademarks of Charles J. Clarke III. NO reproduction in any form is allowed.

# Bulls, Owls, Lambs and Tigers®: Personality Selling™

HE RESPONDED BY

### ANSWERING MY QUESTION WITH A QUESTION.

(AN OFTEN-USED "TORTURE-DEVICE" IN SELLING)

HE SAID, WHICH OF THESE TWO TELEVISIONS, THAT YOU SEE, GIVE THE BEST AND MOST CLEAR PICTURE? HE SAID THIS, USING THE TELEVISION I HAD PICKED OUT AND A NON-FLAT SCREEN, NON-HIGH-DEFINITION TELEVISION SITTING NEXT TO IT.

I RESPONDED THAT OBVIOUSLY THE FLAT SCREEN GAVE THE BETTER PICTURE AND THAT'S WHY I WANTED IT! I SAID, "HOW MUCH IS THIS HIGH-DEFINITION TELEVISION SET WITH THE EXTRA "SURROUND SOUND" SYSTEM?"

### HE DID NOT ANSWER MY QUESTION!

HE SAID, "WELL, THAT BRINGS ME TO MY SURROUND SOUND DEMONSTRATION." (THIS DEMONSTRATION TOOK 5 MINUTES AND 10 SECONDS.) I WAS NUMB WITH DISBELIEF, THINKING (SILENTLY), "THIS IS PURE TORTURE!"

HE SAID, **"THIS SOUNDS GREAT, DOESN'T IT?"** THIS IS, OF COURSE, ANOTHER **TORTURE DEVICE CALLED "THE TIE DOWN"** (ISN'T IT, WASN'T IT, WON'T THEY, DOESN'T IT, ETC). TIE DOWNS ARE "OK" WHEN USED SPARINGLY AND AT THE RIGHT TIME. THIS WAS NOT THE RIGHT TIME.

TWENTY-SEVEN MINUTES FROM THE TIME I WALKED IN, I STILL DIDN'T KNOW THE ANSWER TO MY BASIC TWO QUESTIONS,

1) HOW MUCH FOR EVERYTHING
   AND
2) CAN I GET IT DELIVERED TOMORROW?

WHEN THE SALESPERSON SAID, "I HAVE JUST ONE MORE THING TO TELL YOU," I JUST HAD TO LEAVE, BY "MAKING UP" SOME REASON TO LEAVE.

---

**TORTURE/TORTURE/TORTURE**

---

© 2021 Charles J. Clarke III. "Bulls, Owls, Lambs and Tigers®" is a registered federal trademark of Charles J. Clarke III since 1988. Personality Selling™ and BOLT™ are Trademarks of Charles J. Clarke III. NO reproduction in any form is allowed.

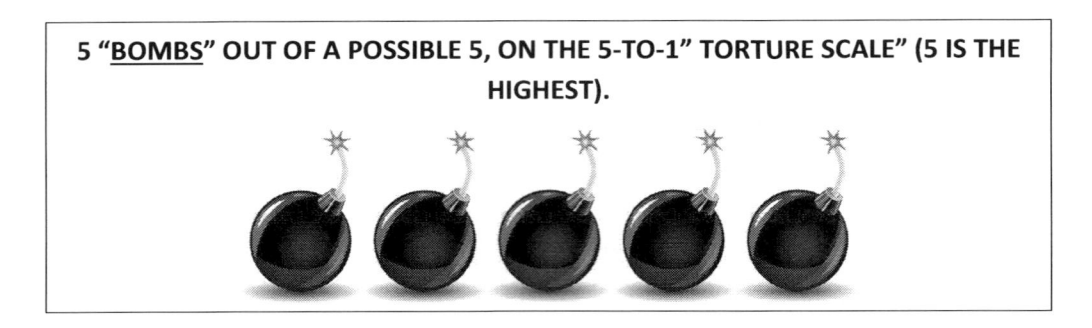

# Bulls, Owls, Lambs and Tigers®: Personality Selling™

> 5 "BOMBS" OUT OF A POSSIBLE 5, ON THE 5-TO-1" TORTURE SCALE" (5 IS THE HIGHEST).

BY ME LEAVING, WHO LOST OUT ON THAT?

I DID (I WAS THE ONE THAT WAS "DIRECTLY" TORTURED), THE SALESMAN, THE SALES MANAGER, AND THE COMPANY BECAUSE OF **LOST SALES AND LOST PROFIT**.

MY FAMILY DID OK! I TOOK THE MONEY INSTEAD TO PURCHASE TICKETS TO HAWAII! (NOT BAD!) TO SEE OUR DAUGHTER TIFFANY, AN ELEMENTARY SCHOOL TEACHER AT THAT TIME, IN HAWAII, SO WE COULD MEET UP WITH HER. SHE IS NOW MARRIED AND TEACHES IN THE TAMPA BAY, FLORIDA AREA.

## MORE EXAMPLES

WE, AS BUYERS, ARE "TORTURED" BECAUSE OF PRECONCEIVED "LIES AND MYTHS" SALESPEOPLE HAVE BEEN TAUGHT THROUGH THE YEARS.

1) THE BUYER WANTS THE PRICE RIGHT AWAY BUT THE SALESPERSON WON'T GIVE IT TO HIM OR HER.
2) THE SALESPERSON IS TOO EMOTIONAL AND BUBBLY FOR A NON-BUBBLY AND NON-EMOTIONAL BUYER.
3) THE SALESPERSON IS TOO "STOIC" FOR AN EMOTIONAL BUYER.
4) ALL OF THE MYTHS INCLUDED IN THIS BOOK, PLUS MANY MORE.

YOU GET THE POINT.

THERE ARE 36 LIES AND MYTHS INCLUDED IN THIS BOOK. ALL HAVE THEIR OWN "BUILT-IN TORTURE SYSTEMS." YOU WILL SEE THAT. I'LL POINT SOME OF THEM OUT, AS WE GO ALONG.

AGAIN, WHAT ARE SOME EXAMPLES THAT YOU HAVE EXPERIENCED? I'D LOVE TO HEAR THEM.

ON ALL THOSE 36 QUESTIONS WHICH YOU PUT A "YES" TO, I'M SUGGESTING THAT'S YOUR WAY OF TORTURING SOME BUYERS, WITHOUT EVEN REALIZING IT.

YOUR THOUGHTS?

# NOTES

THINGS I AGREE WITH

THINGS I DISAGREE WITH

THINGS I NEED TO WORK ON

ACTION PLAN FOR ME

## CHAPTER 4

LET'S LOOK AT THE FIRST QUESTION AND SEE HOW OUR OPINIONS COULD AFFECT OUR CLOSING RATIO AND PERFORMANCE.

THEN BEFORE WE EXAMINE THE OTHER QUESTIONS, WE WILL GO BACK AND TAKE A LOOK AT MY LIFE-LONG WORK OF "BULLS, OWLS, LAMBS AND TIGERS®: PERSONALITY SELLING™" TO SEE WHY MY ANSWERS ARE ALWAYS NO.

## LIE/MYTH #1: WE NEED TO EARN THE RIGHT TO CLOSE.

IF YOU PUT "YES," LOOK AT THE RESTRICTIONS YOU PUT ON YOURSELF. YES, I KNOW MOST INDUSTRIES STRESS THAT YOU HAVE TO "EARN THE RIGHT TO CLOSE" (ONE OF THE LIES/MYTHS WE HAVE BEEN TAUGHT), BUT ISN'T THAT "SUBJECTIVE?" WHAT DOES IT MEAN TO "EARN THE RIGHT?"

THIS IS MY BELIEF AND THE BELIEF OF MOST "MASTER CLOSERS" (THE BEST OF THE BEST IN YOUR INDUSTRY).

## A SALESPERSON HAS "EARNED THE RIGHT TO CLOSE" IF THE BUYER WALKS INTO THEIR PLACE OF BUSINESS OR IS ALLOWED TO WALK INTO THEIR PLACE OF BUSINESS.

LOOK AT THE DIFFERENCE BETWEEN THESE 2 OPINIONS:

1) HAVING TO EARN THE RIGHT TO CLOSE, OR

2) CLOSING EVERYONE, NO MATTER IF YOU HAVE EARNED THE RIGHT TO DO SO OR NOT. (CLOSING HERE DOES NOT NECESSARILY MEAN THEY BUY, BUT THAT YOU <u>ASKED</u> THEM TO BUY.)

**Bulls, Owls, Lambs and Tigers®: Personality Selling™**

MY OPINION AND THE OPINION OF MASTER CLOSERS IS:

> # "CLOSE EVERYONE," WHETHER YOU HAVE "EARNED" IT OR NOT.

THE OPINION OF THIS BOOK IS:

"CLOSING IS THE MOST IMPORTANT PART OF THE SELLING PROCESS," MORE IMPORTANT THAN ANY OTHER ASPECT, WITH ONE "CAVEAT,"

> # CLOSE ACCORDING TO "THEIR" PERSONALITY, BUT CLOSE EVERYONE!

CLOSING MEANS TO "ATTEMPT" TO CLOSE.

"IT'S ALL IN THE PRESENTATION – YOU WON'T OFFEND ANYONE."

JUMPING AHEAD, I AM RECOMMENDING THAT YOU 100% OF THE TIME, ALL THE TIME WITH EVERYONE, ALWAYS, NO EXCEPTIONS, ASK EVERYONE "WHAT DO YOU THINK (OR FEEL) ABOUT GOING AHEAD WITH THIS TODAY™?

| "THINK" IS FOR BULLS AND OWLS. | "FEEL" IS FOR LAMBS AND TIGERS |
|---|---|

"CLOSING" DOES NOT MEAN YOU WILL ALWAYS HAVE SUCCESS OR THAT THEY WILL ALWAYS SAY YES, BUT IT DOES MEAN YOU WILL AT LEAST ASK THE QUESTION, "WHAT DO YOU THINK ABOUT GOING AHEAD WITH THIS TODAY?"

© 2021 Charles J. Clarke III. "Bulls, Owls, Lambs and Tigers®" is a registered federal trademark of Charles J. Clarke III since 1988. Personality Selling™ and BOLT™ are Trademarks of Charles J. Clarke III. NO reproduction in any form is allowed.

# Bulls, Owls, Lambs and Tigers®: Personality Selling™

THE OPPOSITE OF THIS WOULD BE TO BE "SUBJECTIVE," AND FOR YOU TO CONTEMPLATE AND DECIDE, IF YOU HAD EARNED THE RIGHT TO CLOSE. YOUR SUBJECTIVE OPINION COULD BE:

1) DID I DO THE ENTIRE CRITICAL PATH OF SELLING?

2) DID I GIVE THEM ALL THE INFORMATION THEY NEEDED?

3) WERE THEY A "BE BACK," WAS IT THEIR FIRST TIME IN, OR WAS IT MY FIRST TIME IN TO THEM?

4) WERE THEY QUALIFIED?

MORE ON THAT LATER, BUT FOR NOW I BELIEVE (KNOW) IT IS A MYTH, THAT WE NEED TO EARN THE RIGHT TO CLOSE.

> **I WOULD "RATHER" EARN THE RIGHT TO CLOSE AND DO ALL THE STEPS OF THE CRITICAL PATH OF SELLING, BUT IF I DON'T, I'M CLOSING ANYWAY.**
>
> **CHARLES J. CLARKE III**

IF YOU HAD PUT "YES" TO THIS, HAVE I DONE ANYTHING TO CHANGE YOUR OPINION TO "NO?"

---

THIS LIE/MYTH IS ALSO ABOUT TORTURING THE SALES MANAGER OR OWNER OF THE COMPANY, BECAUSE IT REPRESENTS THE **LOST SALE,** SOMETIMES AS MUCH AS

**50% LOST SALES, OR MORE!**

THAT IS TORTURE FOR THE COMPANY!

# NOTES

THINGS I AGREE WITH

THINGS I DISAGREE WITH

THINGS I NEED TO WORK ON

ACTION PLAN FOR ME

## CHAPTER 5

> # LIE/MYTH #2: IT IS OF UTMOST IMPORTANCE TO TALK ABOUT SOCIAL FIRST, THEN POSSIBLE BUSINESS LATER.

THIS AND THE FOLLOWING QUESTIONS HAVE TO DO WITH MY "BULLS, OWLS, LAMBS AND TIGERS®."

BULLS AND OWLS, MY TWO ANIMALS THAT ARE LESS SOCIAL AND SHOW LESS EMOTION, TELL US THAT THEY REALLY DO NOT WANT SOCIAL FIRST. THEY BOTH WANT BUSINESS FIRST AND THEY ACCOUNT FOR APPROXIMATELY 50% OF THE POPULATION.

A GOOD MIND SET IS APPROXIMATELY 25% OF THE POPULATION IS REPRESENTED BY EACH ANIMAL PERSONALITY. ASK AROUND! ASK OTHERS! LOOK AT YOUR OWN EXPERIENCES!

AGAIN, MOST BOOKS AND SPEAKERS SAY, "BUILD RAPPORT," BY GETTING TO KNOW THE BUYER FIRST, OFFERING EVERYONE WATER OR COFFEE, ETC. BULLS AND OWLS HAVE A HIGHER PROBABILITY OF SAYING "NO," TO YOUR COFFEE, ETC. BECAUSE THEY JUST WANT BUSINESS FIRST AND SOCIAL LATER (IF AT ALL).

### EXAMPLE

SALESPERSON SAYS, "I JUST MADE A FRESH POT OF COFFEE. WOULD YOU LIKE SOME?"

THE BULL SAYS "NO."

THE SALESPERSON SAYS, "OH, COME ON, DON'T YOU LIKE COFFEE?"

THE POTENTIAL BULL BUYER ACTUALLY STARTS TO GET IRRITATED AND ASKS, "WHAT'S THE PRICE OF THIS?" (POINTING TO SOMETHING)

DO YOU, AS THE READER, AGREE OR DISAGREE WITH WHAT I'M SAYING?

I'M SUGGESTING THAT APPROXIMATELY 50% OF ALL POTENTIAL BUYERS ARE BULLS AND OWLS, WHO WANT BUSINESS FIRST RATHER THAN SOCIAL FIRST, AND WHO ACTUALLY RESENT YOUR EMPHASIS ON SOCIAL FIRST.

IF YOU ARE FAMILIAR WITH MY "BULLS, OWLS, LAMBS AND TIGERS®," THEN YOU KNOW WHAT I AM SAYING IS "SPOT ON." TRUE.

## Bulls, Owls, Lambs and Tigers®: Personality Selling™

ASK 10 PEOPLE AT RANDOM, OR EVEN IN YOUR OWN COMPANY, AND YOU WILL FIND APPROXIMATELY HALF WILL SAY THEY <u>DON'T WANT</u> SOCIAL FIRST AND THEY BELIEVE THESE 37 LIES AND MYTHS ARE JUST THAT, "LIES AND MYTHS."

FOR BULLS AND OWLS, INSISTING ON TALKING SOCIAL FIRST, IS REPORTED BY THEM AS A <u>FOUR</u> ON A FIVE-TO-ONE "TORTURE SCALE."

**FOR OWLS AND BULLS**

# NOTES

THINGS I AGREE WITH

THINGS I DISAGREE WITH

THINGS I NEED TO WORK ON

ACTION PLAN FOR ME

# Bulls, Owls, Lambs and Tigers®: Personality Selling™

## CHAPTER 6

> # LIE/MYTH #3: IT IS OF UTMOST IMPORTANCE TO SELL THE CONCEPT OF THE "COMPANY'S VISION," AT THE VERY BEGINNING.

MOST EVERY PUBLIC COMPANY AND LARGE, INDEPENDENT COMPANIES, WILL PROBABLY CRINGE AT THIS "MYTH." THEY ALL INSIST THAT SELLING THE COMPANY'S VISION MUST BE DONE IN THE VERY BEGINNING, IN ORDER TO SEPARATE THEM FROM THE COMPETITORS.

I'M NOT SAYING THIS ISN'T IMPORTANT. I'M JUST SAYING THAT "TIMING IS EVERYTHING!" ASK YOURSELF (AND OTHERS), IF YOU (OR THEY) WOULD CARE ABOUT, OR WANT TO KNOW ABOUT, THE COMPANY'S STORY IN THE FIRST THREE MINUTES (OR AT ALL)?

- BULLS TELL US "NO."
- TIGERS TELL US THEY WOULDN'T BE PAYING ATTENTION.
- LAMBS WOULD BE POLITE AND LISTEN BUT WOULD RATHER NOT HEAR ABOUT IT IN THE BEGINNING.
- OWLS DO CARE.

SO, APPROXIMATELY 75% OF POTENTIAL BUYERS CONSISTENTLY TELL US THEY DO NOT WANT TO HEAR THE "COMPANY'S STORY" IN THE BEGINNING. SOME BUYERS EVENTUALLY WANT TO HEAR THE STORY. SOME BUYERS DO NOT WANT TO HEAR THE STORY AT ALL. (BY THE WAY, OWLS HAVE ALREADY READ AND RE-READ THE INFORMATION ABOUT YOUR COMPANY, ON YOUR WEB SITE.)

> **SO, SOMETIMES YOU ARE ONLY TALKING TO YOURSELF, (WHICH TIGERS FIND VERY ENTERTAINING.)**

I HAVE MANY COPIES OF SALES TRAINING MANUALS FROM BOTH PUBLIC AND LARGE INDEPENDENT COMPANIES, AND MOST ALL OF THEM STRESS HOW IMPORTANT IT IS TO SHARE THE COMPANY'S STORY IN THE BEGINNING. OF COURSE, THEY DO! THEY ALMOST HAVE TO! AGAIN, TIMING IS EVERYTHING!

# Bulls, Owls, Lambs and Tigers®: Personality Selling™

> **HOWEVER, THE TRUTH IS, IT IS ACTUALLY A "TURN-OFF," TO HEAR THE COMPANY'S STORY IN THE FIRST FEW MINUTES, FOR A LARGE MAJORITY OF BUYERS.**

THE GOOD NEWS IS THAT MOST "MASTER CLOSERS" AND EXCELLENT SALESPEOPLE KNOW THIS AND DON'T PRACTICE THIS IN THE REAL WORLD.

THE BAD NEWS IS THAT WHEN THE "MASTER CLOSER" GETS "MYSTERY SHOPPED," (NOT BEING AWARE THEY ARE EVEN BEING SHOPPED), THEY READ THE BUYER AND DON'T ALWAYS GET "GOOD GRADES" ON THEIR SHOP. DESPITE THE "BAD GRADE," THE MASTER CLOSER SELLS MORE THAN ANYONE ELSE. WHICH IS MORE IMPORTANT?

SOME COMPANIES ARE "INSISTING" THAT THE "COMPANY'S STORY" GO ON FOR ABOUT FIVE MINUTES, RIGHT IN THE BEGINNING. LET'S GET REAL! YES, THERE IS A TIME AND PLACE FOR THE "COMPANY STORY," BUT NOT RIGHT AWAY, AND NOT FOR SO LONG.

THE BEST PLACE FOR IT IS IN THE MIDDLE OF THE CRITICAL PATH OF SELLING (DEMONSTRATION-BOX #5, CHAPTER XXX, MYTH #27.)

WHAT ARE <u>YOUR</u> THOUGHTS ON THIS? SEE CHAPTER VII FOR THE PLACEMENT OF THE "COMPANY STORY."

I HAVE BEEN ABLE TO GUIDE SOME OF THE LARGER, PUBLIC COMPANIES AND LARGE NATIONAL, INDEPENDENT COMPANIES AWAY FROM DOING THE ABOVE, BUT OTHERS CONTINUE TO DO SO. I'M STILL WORKING ON THEM.

> TELLING THE COMPANY'S STORY IN THE BEGINNING AND FOR A LONG TIME IS CERTAINLY A FOUR ON A FIVE-TO-ONE "TORTURE SCALE."
>
> 💣 💣 💣 💣

HAVE YOU EVER EXPERIENCED THAT?

> **YOU CAN'T BUY UNTIL I "TORTURE YOU" WITH TELLING YOU ALL ABOUT OUR COMPANY!**

# NOTES

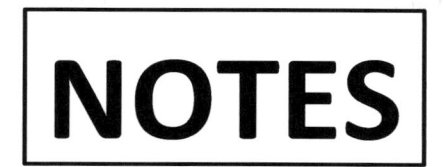

THINGS I AGREE WITH




THINGS I DISAGREE WITH




THINGS I NEED TO WORK ON




ACTION PLAN FOR ME

# CHAPTER 7

## LIE/MYTH #4: OF ALL THE STEPS OF THE CRITICAL PATH OF SELLING, THE OUTRIGHT MOST IMPORTANT STEP IS DEMONSTRATION!

YOU WILL SEE THAT I AM "BIASED" WHEN IT COMES TO SELLING. MY BIAS, NO MATTER WHAT YOU ARE SELLING, IS IN THE DIRECTION OF:

**CLOSING.**

**I BELIEVE "CLOSING" IS ABSOLUTELY THE MOST IMPORTANT STEP OF THE CRITICAL PATH OF SELLING!**

BELOW ARE NOT CHARLES J. CLARKE III'S CRITICAL PATH STEPS. THEY ARE CRITICAL PATH STEPS THAT ARE OVER 100 YEARS OLD AND DATE BACK TO SELLING DURING THE INDUSTRIAL REVOLUTION, IN THE LATE 1800'S.

**OLD, GENERIC CRITICAL PATH OF SELLING**

1) MEET AND GREET

2) QUALIFY
   QUALIFY FOR
   - READY (TIMING)
   - WILLING (PRODUCT)
   - ABLE (FINANCIAL)

3) DEMONSTRATION OF PRODUCT

4) SELECTION PROCESS
   WHAT DO THEY LIKE BEST?

5) OVERCOME OBJECTIONS AND CLOSE THE SALE

**MY VARIATION OF THE CRITICAL PATH OF SALES, AS IT RELATES TO ANY INDUSTRY**

# Bulls, Owls, Lambs and Tigers®: Personality Selling™

1) **MEET AND GREET** – MEET, GREET, AND CONNECT WITH THEIR BOLT™, (THEIR ANIMAL PERSONALITY.) "PACE AND MIRROR" WITH THEM.

2) **QUALIFY** FOR
   - READY: HAVE THEY DECIDED TO PURCHASE SOMETHING SIMILAR TO YOUR PRODUCT OR ARE THEY AT LEAST THINKING ABOUT IT? ABOUT 25% (LAMBS AND OWLS) ARE JUST "LOOKERS" AND REALLY HAVEN'T DECIDED TO ACTUALLY BUY YOUR TYPE OF PRODUCT.
   - WILLING: WILLING IS ALL ABOUT PRODUCT. PRODUCT ALSO INCLUDES THE SALESPERSON.
   - ABLE: FINANCIALLY ABLE

3) **DEMONSTRATION** (EXPLANATION OF YOUR PRODUCT)
DEMONSTRATION IS THE "3$^{RD}$ STEP" OF THE CRITICAL PATH. THIS IS WHY IT REALLY DOES NOT MAKE SENSE FROM A CRITICAL PATH PERSPECTIVE, TO TELL THE COMPANY STORY IN THE FIRST FEW MINUTES. TELL IT LATER, UNDER DEMONSTRATION.

THERE ARE STILL A LOT OF SALESPEOPLE WHO JUST "JUMP IN" AND START TALKING ABOUT THEIR PRODUCT. WORSE YET, IS THE PRESENTATION THAT SAYS, "GO TAKE A LOOK AT OUR PRODUCT," WITHOUT QUALIFYING AT ALL. (THESE SALES PEOPLE USUALLY HAVE A CLOSING RATIO OF A "CLERK" OR "BAD CLERK.")

4) **SELECTION** (OF WHAT THEY WANT)
   1) HOW DO YOU LIKE EVERYTHING YOU HAVE SEEN AND HEARD TODAY?
   2) WHICH ASPECT DID YOU LIKE BEST (FROM MY PRESENTATION?)
   3) WHICH SPECIFIC PRODUCT DID YOU LIKE BEST?

   *I'M JUST USING THE WORD "PRODUCT." SUBSTITUTE THE ACTUAL PRODUCT TO WHICH YOU ARE REFERRING.*

5) **OVERCOMING OBJECTIONS AND CLOSING THE SALE**
   USING THE RIGHT CLOSING METHODOLOGY FOR EACH PERSONALITY USING KILLER CLOSES FOR EACH PERSONALITY™

© 2021 Charles J. Clarke III. "Bulls, Owls, Lambs and Tigers®" is a registered federal trademark of Charles J. Clarke III since 1988. Personality Selling™ and BOLT™ are Trademarks of Charles J. Clarke III. NO reproduction in any form is allowed.

# Bulls, Owls, Lambs and Tigers®: Personality Selling™

## THE PART OF THE CRITICAL PATH OF SELLING EACH ANIMAL PERSONALITY NEEDS/WANTS

- **OWLS** – NEED/WANT DEMONSTRATION THE <u>MOST</u>
- **LAMBS** – LIKE DEMONSTRATION IF THEY ARE "CORDIAL" DEMONSTRATIONS
- **TIGERS** – NEED DEMONSTRATION THE <u>MOST</u>, BUT ALSO WANT IT THE <u>LEAST</u>
- **BULLS** – NEED/WANT DEMONSTRATION THE <u>LEAST</u>

BASED ON WHAT BUYERS HAVE TOLD US THROUGH THE YEARS, SOME BUYERS ACTUALLY FIND IT "OFFENSIVE," HOW MUCH DETAIL IS SPENT BY "OWL" SALESPEOPLE ON "MUNDANE" AND "OVER-DETAILED" PRESENTATIONS. FOR EXAMPLE:

> IN DEMONSTRATING THE KITCHEN IN A MODEL HOME, A SALESPERSON SAYS,
> **"THIS IS THE KITCHEN." – (DUH!)**

WE ACTUALLY HAVE ON OUR "MYSTERY SHOPS," STATEMENTS BY SALESPEOPLE AS THEY STEP INTO THE KITCHEN, "THIS IS THE KITCHEN," AND AS THEY GO INTO THE BATHROOM, "THIS IS THE BATHROOM."

AS A BUYER, WE HAVE PROBABLY ALL EXPERIENCED THAT, HAVEN'T WE? (HIGH TORTURE)

BULLS HAVE A HIGH PROBABILITY OF WANTING TO SEE THE PRODUCT ON THEIR OWN, OFTEN SAYING, "I JUST WANT TO SEE IT ON MY OWN." WE CAN SAY SOMETHING LIKE, "IF IT'S ALL RIGHT WITH YOU, I WOULD LIKE TO START YOU OFF BY DEMONSTRATING SOME SPECIFIC ITEMS. AFTER THAT, I CAN LEAVE YOU ALONE. WOULD THAT BE ALL RIGHT?"

THEN SOME OF THE BULLS WILL ACTUALLY "ALLOW" YOU TO STAY WITH THEM; SOMETIMES KEEPING THEIR DISTANCE.

IF YOU GIVE THE EXACT "WORD FOR WORD" DEMONSTRATION OF YOUR PRODUCT THAT IS OFTEN RECOMMENDED, YOU WILL SOUND LIKE A "ROBOT," AND BE BUSTED BY BULLS AND OTHERS FOR DOING THAT.

> **YES, DEMONSTRATION IS, OF COURSE, VERY IMPORTANT. YET, YOU COULD HAVE THE BEST DEMONSTRATION EVER, BUT IF YOU DON'T CLOSE, IT'S ALL FOR NAUGHT.**

NOTE TO OWL SALESPEOPLE: NOT EVERYONE WANTS TO HEAR ALL THE WONDERFUL KNOWLEDGE YOU HAVE.

# Bulls, Owls, Lambs and Tigers®: Personality Selling™

> **<u>ALL</u> THE STEPS OF THE CRICITAL PATHS ARE IMPORTANT, BUT THE MOST IMPORTANT IS THE CLOSING.**

YOUR THOUGHTS?

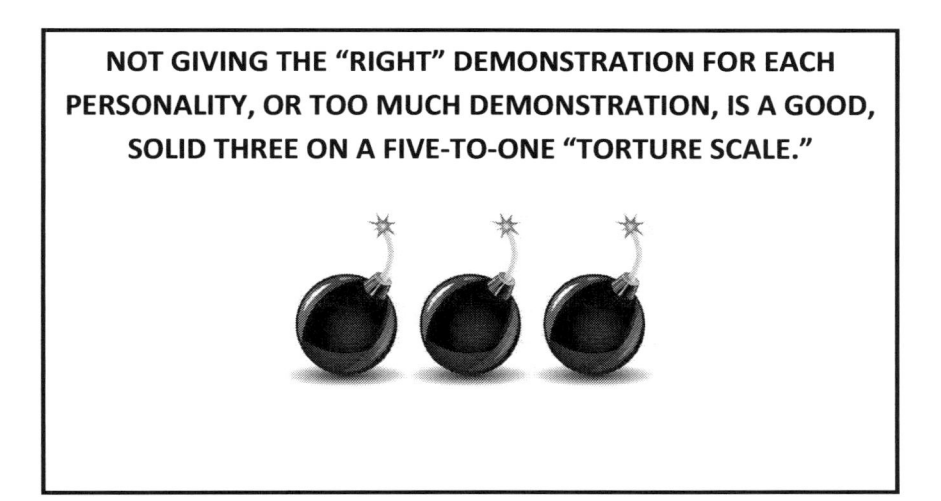

> **NOT GIVING THE "RIGHT" DEMONSTRATION FOR EACH PERSONALITY, OR TOO MUCH DEMONSTRATION, IS A GOOD, SOLID THREE ON A FIVE-TO-ONE "TORTURE SCALE."**

# NOTES

THINGS I AGREE WITH



THINGS I DISAGREE WITH



THINGS I NEED TO WORK ON



ACTION PLAN FOR ME

Bulls, Owls, Lambs and Tigers®: Personality Selling™

## CHAPTER 8

> # LIE/MYTH #5: IT WOULD BE TOO PUSHY TO, 100% OF THE TIME, ASK FOR THE SALE.

ALMOST EVERY SALES MANAGER THROUGHOUT THE WORLD STRESSES TO THEIR SALES STAFF, "ASK EVERYONE FOR THE SALE." (CLOSE EVERYONE.)

HOWEVER, WHEN COMPANIES DO MYSTERY SHOPPING *(WHETHER THEY USE OUR MYSTERY SHOPPING COMPANY OR NOT)* THE

> **ABSOLUTE MOST NEGLECTED STEP IS CLOSING.**

QUESTION "DID THE SALESPERSON ASK YOU TO BUY?"

ANSWER "NO"

AGAIN:

> **IN MY BIASED OPINION, CLOSING IS ABSOLUTELY THE SINGLE MOST IMPORTANT AND NEGLECTED STEP IN SELLING. YES, ALL THE STEPS IN THE CRITICAL PATH ARE IMPORTANT, BUT THE MOST IMPORTANT IS CLOSING.**
>
> **CHARLES J. CLARKE III**

WHAT ARE YOUR THOUGHTS ON THIS?

IN THIS CHAPTER, I AM GOING TO TRY TO "CLOSE" ON YOU, TO DO A CERTAIN TASK FOR 90 DAYS. THEN IF IT WORKS, YOU CAN "RE-UP" FOR MORE COMMITMENT.

## Bulls, Owls, Lambs and Tigers®: Personality Selling™

HERE IS WHAT I'M ASKING YOU TO COMMIT. (SOME OF YOU WILL/SOME OF YOU WON'T. THAT'S OKAY.)

WILL YOU COMMIT TO ASK <u>EVERYONE, ALL THE TIME, NO EXCEPTIONS, ALWAYS,</u> (FOR 90 DAYS) (HOW ABOUT FOREVER?)

---

### "WHAT DO YOU THINK ABOUT GOING AHEAD WITH THIS TODAY?"

---

*(WITH A LAMB AND TIGER YOU CAN SUBSTITUTE THE WORD "FEEL" INSTEAD OF "THINK.")*

I RAN ACROSS SOMEONE'S WEBSITE WHO SOMETIMES GIVES ADVICE AND HE MADE THE STATEMENT ONLINE, THAT THE WORST CLOSE IS "WHAT DO YOU THINK ABOUT GOING AHEAD WITH THIS TODAY?" I BELIEVE HE MUST HAVE BEEN REFERRING TO MY WORK.

HE WENT ON TO SAY THAT A PERSON OR COUPLE BUYS WITH "FEELING, NOT THINKING." (SEE QUESTION #22 AND LIE/MYTH #22)

WHAT HE WAS EXPRESSING WAS HIS LACK OF KNOWLEDGE OF PERSONALITY SELLING™. OWLS AND BULLS <u>PREFER</u> THE WORD "THINK." THEY "SORT DATA," BY THINKING. EVEN LAMBS AND TIGERS "THINK" ABOUT BUYING.

IT'S REALLY NOT THAT BIG OF A DEAL IF YOU USE "THINK" OR "FEEL." THE BIG DEAL IS FOR YOU TO ASK THE POTENTIAL BUYER, "<u>WHAT DO YOU THINK ABOUT GOING AHEAD WITH THIS TODAY™?</u>" 100% OF THE TIME, FOR THE NEXT 90 DAYS. (SUBSTITUTE "FEEL" WHEN IT IS APPROPRIATE, IF YOU "THINK" THAT IS NECESSARY.)

WILL YOU DO THAT?

SALESPEOPLE WHO <u>HAVE</u> DONE AND WHO <u>ARE</u> DOING THE ABOVE, SEE THEIR SALES IMMEDIATELY INCREASE.

# Bulls, Owls, Lambs and Tigers®: Personality Selling™

LET ME CLARIFY MORE OF WHAT I'M SUGGESTING. I CALL THESE MY FIVE MAGIC QUESTIONS™, TO ASK EVERYONE BEFORE THEY LEAVE (OR YOU LEAVE), USUALLY ABOUT 20 MINUTES INTO THE PRESENTATION.

## THE FIVE MAGIC QUESTIONS

1) HOW DO YOU LIKE EVERYTHING YOU HAVE SEEN OR HEARD TODAY?

2) WHICH PART OF MY PRESENTATION DID YOU LIKE THE BEST?

3) WHICH OF THE "PRODUCTS" I DEMONSTRATED DID YOU LIKE THE BEST? (DON'T CALL IT PRODUCT)

4) WOULD YOU LIKE TO DO BUSINESS WITH US?

5) WHAT DO YOU THINK ABOUT GOING AHEAD WITH THIS TODAY? (THE SILVER BULLET) YOU CAN ACTUALLY SKIP THE FIRST FOUR QUESTIONS AND JUST ASK THE FIFTH ONE, IF APPROPRIATE.

---

**HAVE FUN WITH IT! ASK EVERYONE.**

**"MAKE IT A HABIT."**

---

LET ME ASK YOU A QUESTION, "DID YOU BRUSH YOUR TEETH TODAY?" WHY? SURE, IT IS BECAUSE IT IS GOOD HYGIENE, YOUR TEETH WILL BE WHITER, YOUR BREATH WILL BE BETTER, AND YOU WILL KEEP YOUR TEETH LONGER. HOWEVER, YOU ALSO DID IT BECAUSE, "IT IS A HABIT."

MAKE THIS A HABIT!

# THE CHARLES J. CLARKE III COMMITMENT

I, _____, HEREBY COMMIT TO ASK, "WHAT DO YOU THINK ABOUT GOING AHEAD WITH THIS TODAY," 100% OF THE TIME, ALL OF THE TIME, WITH EVERYONE (NO EXCEPTIONS), FOR THE NEXT 90 DAYS BEGINNING _____.

(MONTH/DATE/YEAR)

_____  _____  _____  _____
SIGNED                    COMPANY                CITY            STATE

_____
                                                        DATE

MAKE A COPY OF THIS PAGE

GIVE A COPY TO YOUR SALES MANAGER AND EMAIL A COPY TO CHARLES J. CLARKE III.

EMAIL = CHARLES@PERSONALITYSELLING.COM (IF YOU WANT TO.)

*THIS IS THE ONLY PAGE IN THE BOOK THAT I GIVE YOU PERMISSION TO COPY. THANK YOU.

CHARLES J. CLARKE III

TO SALES MANAGERS: ON ALL THE OTHER PAGES, PLEASE DO NOT COPY PAGES TO HAND OUT TO YOUR SALESPEOPLE. JUST BUY ENOUGH COPIES OF THIS BOOK TO GIVE TO EVERYONE.

**Bulls, Owls, Lambs and Tigers®: Personality Selling™**

QUIT TRYING TO SECOND GUESS IF IT IS THE RIGHT THING TO DO. JUST DO IT, WITH EVERYONE!

# HERE ARE 7 PSYCHOLOGICAL REASONS WHY YOU MIGHT NOT BE ASKING THE "FIVE MAGIC QUESTIONS"

1) **FEAR OF REJECTION** – (YOU ALSO THINK IT WOULD BE "STUPID" TO DO THIS IN SOME CASES.) (GET OVER IT!)

2) "I DON'T WANT TO BE TOO PUSHY. (GET OVER IT!)

3) MY "JUDGMENT" IS THAT THEY ARE NOT READY TO BE ASKED (SOME EVEN TOLD YOU THAT). (BULLS ARE THE MOST JUDGMENTAL AS SALESPEOPLE).

   A) THEY WEREN'T A BUYER (NOT READY)
   B) DIDN'T LIKE THE PRODUCT (NOT WILLING)
   C) DIDN'T HAVE THE MONEY (NOT ABLE)
   D) SAID THEY NEEDED TO TAKE CARE OF SOMETHING ELSE FIRST
   E) SAID OR THOUGHT THE PRICE WAS TOO HIGH
   F) NEEDED TO HAVE A SPOUSE (OR SOMEONE) TO APPROVE IT
   G) NEED TO THINK IT OVER

"PAD" THEIR OBJECTIONS, SO THEY UNDERSTAND YOU HEARD THE OBJECTION. "I REALLY DID HEAR YOU SAY YOU NEEDED TO HAVE YOUR SPOUSE LOOK AT IT FIRST, BUT I'M COMPELLED TO ASK YOU, ANYWAY, 'WHAT DO YOU THINK ABOUT GOING AHEAD WITH THIS TODAY?'"

YOU CAN "PAD" ANY OBJECTION.

4) I'M NOT READY (I DIDN'T GET A CHANCE TO GIVE MY FULL PRESENTATION) ("I" WOULDN'T BUY UNDER THESE CIRCUMSTANCES)

5) I THINK THEY WILL "BE BACK"

(THE "BE BACK BUS" DOESN'T STOP HERE, IF THEY MEET A CLOSER ALONG THE WAY.)

© 2021 Charles J. Clarke III. "Bulls, Owls, Lambs and Tigers®" is a registered federal trademark of Charles J. Clarke III since 1988. Personality Selling™ and BOLT™ are Trademarks of Charles J. Clarke III. NO reproduction in any form is allowed.

## Bulls, Owls, Lambs and Tigers®: Personality Selling™

6) I DIDN'T FEEL LIKE IT (IT'S JUST NOT MY STYLE) (THAT'S NOT HOW I ROLL) (GET OVER IT!)

7) I JUST PLAIN "FORGOT" TO ASK. (THAT'S WHY YOU NEED THE TENT CARD.)

GO THROUGH THESE SEVEN AND RANK THE TOP 3 THAT GET IN YOUR WAY THE MOST. WHAT IS YOUR #1, #2 AND #3? WRITE THEM DOWN, SO YOU CAN OVERCOME THESE REASONS. OFTEN A PERSON'S BULL, OWL, LAMB AND TIGER® SHOWS UP IN TERMS OF THE REASON THEY DON'T ASK.

IN MY PERSONAL TAILOR-MADE SEMINARS FOR COMPANIES, I ASK "WHICH GETS IN YOUR WAY THE MOST?" LAMBS AND OWLS HAVE #1 AND #2 SHOW UP THE MOST IN THEIR TOP THREE; SOMETIMES #6.

BULLS HAVE #3 SHOW UP THE MOST (USUALLY). IT'S THEIR #1 REASON BECAUSE BULLS ARE SO OPINIONATED, THEY THINK THEY ARE ALWAYS RIGHT.

OWLS HAVE #4 SHOW UP THE MOST IN THEIR TOP THREE.

ALL FOUR ANIMALS HAVE #5 SHOW UP.

TIGERS HAVE #7 SHOW UP THE MOST.

# LET'S LOOK AT REASON #5 "THEY WILL BE BACK."

WHAT IS YOUR "BEEN BACK™" RATIO? NOT YOUR "BE BACK" RATIO, BUT RATHER, YOUR "BEEN BACK™" RATIO.

ALLOW ME TO DIGRESS. THEN I WILL ANSWER THAT. A "BE BACK" IS, OF COURSE, SOMEONE WHO SAYS THEY WILL BE BACK. SOMETIMES THEY DO COME BACK, AND SOMETIMES THEY DON'T. MOST COMPANIES USE A "BE BACK" RATIO IN TERMS OF CALCULATING RETURN VISITS.

THE AVERAGE "BE BACK" RATIO (RETURN VISITS) WITH COMPANIES APPEARS TO BE ABOUT 20%. THE REASON FOR THIS BEING SO HIGH IS BECAUSE "BE BACKS" CAN BE COUNTED TWICE, OR 3, 4 OR 5 TIMES IF THE PROSPECTIVE BUYER KEEPS RETURNING.

© 2021 Charles J. Clarke III. "Bulls, Owls, Lambs and Tigers®" is a registered federal trademark of Charles J. Clarke III since 1988. Personality Selling™ and BOLT™ are Trademarks of Charles J. Clarke III. NO reproduction in any form is allowed.

**Bulls, Owls, Lambs and Tigers®: Personality Selling™**

WHICH ANIMAL PERSONALITIES DO YOU THINK RETURN THE MOST? THE LEAST?

> **LAMBS AND OWLS RETURN THE MOST. BULLS USUALLY ONLY COME BACK, POSSIBLY ONE MORE TIME, JUST TO SEE IF THEY CAN GET A BETTER PRICE.**

> **TIGERS VERY RARELY EVER COME BACK AT ALL. THEY "PREFER" TO BUY THE FIRST DAY (NO MATTER WHAT THE PRODUCT.)**

DO YOU BELIEVE THE PREVIOUS STATEMENT?
IF YOU ARE AN OWL, I KNOW YOU REALLY DON'T BELIEVE IT, AT THIS POINT IN TIME.

ASK TIGERS!

> **"BEEN BACK" RATIOS**

WHERE "BE BACKS" CAN BE COUNTED MORE THAN ONCE, A "BEEN BACK" IS ONLY COUNTED ONCE.

> **IF YOU HAVE 100 PEOPLE COME IN (NO MATTER HOW LONG IT TAKES FOR THAT NUMBER TO COME IN), HOW MANY OF THOSE 100 WILL <u>EVER</u> COME BACK?**

PLEASE WRITE THIS NUMBER DOWN. TAKE A MOMENT TO THINK ABOUT IT BUT WRITE SOME NUMBER DOWN BEFORE YOU PROCEED. TURN THAT INTO A PERCENTAGE SINCE IT WAS BASED ON 100.

© 2021 Charles J. Clarke III. "Bulls, Owls, Lambs and Tigers®" is a registered federal trademark of Charles J. Clarke III since 1988. Personality Selling™ and BOLT™ are Trademarks of Charles J. Clarke III. NO reproduction in any form is allowed.

**Bulls, Owls, Lambs and Tigers®: Personality Selling™**

IN OUR SEMINARS, SOME SALESPEOPLE (NOT MANY) ANSWER THAT THEY THINK THEY HAVE 50% "BEEN BACKS." THEY DON'T!

> ## THE NATIONAL AVERAGE (AS FAR AS WE CAN DISCERN) OF "BEEN BACK" RATIOS" IS 8% TO 10%.

OUT OF EVERY 100 PEOPLE, 90% TO 92% NEVER RETURN. AS MENTIONED, SOME OF THE "BE BACKS" COME BACK EVEN 5 OR 6 TIMES, SO A SALESPERSON STARTS TO THINK THEY HAVE MORE "BEEN BACKS," THAN THEY REALLY DO.

> ## 90% to 92% NEVER COME BACK

AGAIN, IN MY SEMINARS, SOME SALESPEOPLE PROFESSIONALLY "DEBATE" THESE "BEEN BACK" NUMBERS, SAYING, "I HAVE TWICE THAT MANY OF 8% AND 10%." OK! LET'S SAY YOU DO HAVE A 16% TO 20% "BEEN BACK" RATIO.

> ## READJUSTED, THAT STILL MEANS 80% TO 84% OF PEOPLE ARE NEVER COMING BACK!

DOES THAT CONVINCE YOU THAT YOU SHOULD BE ASKING EVERYONE, "WHAT DO YOU THINK ABOUT GOING AHEAD WITH THIS TODAY?"

WHAT DO YOU HAVE TO LOSE?

THE ANSWER IS THAT YOU HAVE "NOTHING TO LOSE" EXCEPT, OF COURSE, THE SALE.

YOU HAVE EVERYTHING TO WIN BY ASKING IT.

WILL YOU MAKE (SIGN) THE COMMITMENT ON ONE OF THE PREVIOUS PAGES, OR HAVE YOU ALREADY SIGNED IT?

"THE FUTURE IS YOURS™."

---

© 2021 Charles J. Clarke III. "Bulls, Owls, Lambs and Tigers®" is a registered federal trademark of Charles J. Clarke III since 1988. Personality Selling™ and BOLT™ are Trademarks of Charles J. Clarke III. NO reproduction in any form is allowed.

# Bulls, Owls, Lambs and Tigers®: Personality Selling™

GIVE A COPY TO YOUR SALES MANAGER AND SEND US A COPY OF YOUR COMMITMENT, ALONG WITH YOUR "THOUGHTS," ABOUT WHAT I HAVE BEEN SHARING WITH YOU.

***TIGERS REALLY DON'T CARE ABOUT ALL THESE PERCENTAGES AND PROBABLY SKIPPED OVER THIS.***

ONE LAST THOUGHT ON THIS SUBJECT OF ASKING EVERYONE IF THEY WANT TO BUY.

---

**START IMAGINING HOW MUCH BUSINESS YOU HAVE <u>RECENTLY LOST</u> OR TOTALLY LOST FOR YOUR COMPANY AND FOR YOURSELF, BY NOT ASKING FOR THE SALE.**

---

HOW MUCH MONEY DID THAT END UP BEING, THAT YOU LOST?

---

**THAT IS SELF-TORTURE <u>AND</u> COMPANY TORTURE.**

---

© 2021 Charles J. Clarke III. "Bulls, Owls, Lambs and Tigers®" is a registered federal trademark of Charles J. Clarke III since 1988. Personality Selling™ and BOLT™ are Trademarks of Charles J. Clarke III. NO reproduction in any form is allowed.

# NOTES

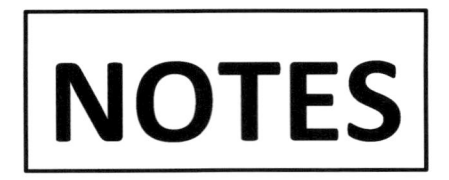

THINGS I AGREE WITH

THINGS I DISAGREE WITH

THINGS I NEED TO WORK ON

ACTION PLAN FOR ME

# Bulls, Owls, Lambs and Tigers®: Personality Selling™

## CHAPTER 9

> # LIE/MYTH #6: IT IS RARE FOR SOMEONE TO "BUY" (GIVE A CHECK AND SIGN THE CONTRACT) THE FIRST TIME THEY SEE YOUR PRESENTATION OR YOUR PRODUCT.

IF YOU ORIGINALLY PUT "YES" TO THIS STATEMENT, WHAT WERE YOUR REASONS? WERE YOUR REASONS SOMETHING LIKE:

1) "PEOPLE DON'T BUY THE FIRST DAY,"
2) "THEY NEED MORE INFORMATION AND RESEARCH TO MAKE SUCH A BIG DECISION,"
3) "THERE'S TOO MUCH COMPETITION OUT THERE FROM WHICH PEOPLE CAN CHOOSE,"
4) "IT RARELY HAPPENS," AND/OR
5) "OUR PRODUCT TAKES A LONG TIME TO SELL. IT IS VERY INTRICATE."

ACTUALLY, THE MAIN REASON WHY <u>YOU</u> MIGHT HAVE SAID, "YES," TO IT BEING "RARE," WAS BECAUSE <u>YOU</u> WOULDN'T DO IT THE FIRST DAY AND <u>YOU</u> WOULD NEED MORE TIME AND RESEARCH. YOU THINK IT'S ABOUT <u>YOU</u>, NOT THEM, AND IT REALLY SHOULD BE IN REVERSE (ABOUT THEM AND NOT YOU).

IF <u>YOU</u> WOULD <u>NOT</u> BUY THE FIRST DAY, YOU PROBABLY WILL NOT BELIEVE THIS. (I HAVE ALREADY MENTIONED THIS.)

YET, IN SALES, A VERY HIGH PERCENTAGE OF SALESPEOPLE SAY IT IS RARE FOR SOMEONE TO BUY THE FIRST DAY (DEPENDING ON THEIR PRODUCT).

> **APPROXIMATELY 50% OF ALL THE POPULATION WE SURVEY, SAY THEY <u>HAVE</u> "BOUGHT" THE FIRST DAY, NO MATTER WHAT THE PRODUCT IS.**
> **(MAINLY TIGERS AND BULLS)**

# Bulls, Owls, Lambs and Tigers®: Personality Selling™

**MASTER CLOSERS HAVE ⅓ TO ½ OF ALL THEIR SALES SOLD THE FIRST DAY.**

DO YOU BELIEVE THAT?

SOME POTENTIAL BUYERS SAY THEY DIDN'T BUY, BECAUSE EITHER THE SALESPERSON DIDN'T ASK THEM, OR THE SALESPERSON <u>CONVINCED</u> THEM NOT TO BUY. "TAKE YOUR TIME, THERE IS NO NEED TO RUSH INTO THIS,

> "IF YOU DON'T GET MANY SALES DONE THE FIRST DAY, IT MAY BE BECAUSE YOU ARE NOT EXPECTING IT."
>
> CHARLES J. CLARKE III

YOUR THOUGHTS?

> **DEPENDING ON WHAT YOU ARE SELLING, IF AT LEAST 33% TO 50% OF YOUR TOTAL SALES ARE <u>NOT</u> DONE THE FIRST DAY YOU MIGHT BE (PROBABLY ARE) MISSING <u>ALL</u> THE TIGER BUYERS, AND A GOOD PORTION OF THE BULL BUYERS.**

SEE THE LETTER FROM JOHN CRISTY, ON THE NEXT PAGE.

REMEMBER, A GOOD MIND-SET IS THAT THE POPULATION IS DIVIDED INTO ABOUT 25% BULLS, 25% OWLS, 25% LAMBS & 25% TIGERS.

SEND US <u>YOUR</u> TESTIMONIALS TO BE INCLUDED IN <u>VOLUME II</u>, "LIES AND MYTHS WE HAVE BEEN TAUGHT IN SELLING."

> **NO MATTER WHAT YOU ARE SELLING: AT LEAST 1/3 TO 1/2 OF ALL YOUR SALES "COULD BE"/"SHOULD BE" DONE THE FIRST DAY, AND THAT IS "NOT RARE."**

# Bulls, Owls, Lambs and Tigers®: Personality Selling™

To: Charles J. Clarke III

From: John Christy

Subject: Thank You

Hello Charles,

It was great to see you again. I just wanted to take a moment and Thank You for sharing your philosophy of selling which has impacted my selling career. During what most would consider turbulent times I was able to sell 88 homes during the past year.

It was a mix of townhouses and detached single family ranging in price from $170,000-$300,000. My conversion ratio on the townhome mix was 1 out of 3 and in the detached single family it ended up being 1 out of 6. And it will come as no surprise to you that 37% of these customers purchased on the first day, just like you recommend.

If I were to have listened to the old myths like:

1) "You have to earn the right to close,"
2) Tell the Builder Story first before you qualify,
3) "People don't buy the first day,"
4) "Everyone wants a relationship," etc.

I would have not sold even half the number of homes I did, listening to traditional myths.

Charles you are truly the Master Professor who helped turn me into another one of your Master Closers. Your methodology has empowered me to shorten my sales cycle and create a high-level customer experience, because I now take the time to relate to each individual's personality (their BOLT™).

Thanks again to you and my Sales Manager Briggs Napier for providing you to me, and for training material that makes a difference in the bottom line of the student not just the teacher.

Looking forward to another great year. YO LET'S DO IT!

Expect Success!

John J. Christy

Raleigh, N.C.

88 homes sold in ONE YEAR!

# Bulls, Owls, Lambs and Tigers®: Personality Selling™

> **EXAMPLE OF SELLING, THE FIRST DAY, A MULTI-MILLION DOLLAR CHEMICAL CONTRACT, THAT USUALLY TAKES ONE YEAR OR MORE TO QUOTE AND SELL**

I HAD GIVEN A SEMINAR TO A DIVISION OF "YPO" – (YOUNG PRESIDENTS ORGANIZATION). SHORTLY AFTER THE SEMINAR, ONE OF THE ATTENDEES, JON OUTCALT, INVITED ME TO COME INTO HIS TWO COMPANIES, FEDERAL PROCESS AND FEDCHEM OUT OF CLEVELAND, OHIO.

FEDERAL PROCESS IS A LEADING SUPPLIER OF THREAD SEALANTS, INK GELLANTS, GREASE THICKENERS, AND LUBRICANTS. FEDCHEM IS A LONGER-TERM CHEMICAL CONTRACTOR SELLING MULTI-MILLION DOLLAR, <u>HIGHLY INVOLVED</u> CHEMICAL CONTRACTS.

DURING MY ALL-DAY SEMINAR WITH THEM, ON "BULLS, OWLS, LAMBS AND TIGERS®: PERSONALITY SELLING™," I GOT TO THE PART ABOUT 100% OF THE TIME ASKING FOR THE SALE, THE FIRST TIME A SALESPERSON IS WITH THE CUSTOMER.

I WAS IMMEDIATELY TOLD THIS DID <u>NOT</u> APPLY TO THE FEDCHEM BUSINESS, BECAUSE SOME OF THEIR SALES WERE SO INVOLVED AND INTRICATE THAT THE SALES SOMETIMES TOOK WELL OVER A YEAR OR MORE TO CLOSE.

I CONTINUED, "AFTER YOUR PRESENTATION, AND AFTER YOU ASK, 'WHAT DO YOU THINK ABOUT GOING AHEAD WITH THIS TODAY?' AND AFTER THEY SAY, 'NO,' YOU CAN WRITE THE FOLLOWING ON THE ORDER FORM/CONTRACT:

> **"THIS CONTRACT IS <u>SUBJECT TO</u> YOU AGREEING TO ALL THE SPECIFICS, DETAILS, AND INGREDIENTS OF THE FINAL CONTRACT, AND IS SUBJECT TO YOU AGREEING TO THE FINAL PRICE."**

YOU CAN, OF COURSE, USE YOUR OWN WORDS FOR THIS "SUBJECT TO" OR "CONTINGENT UPON."

IT WAS ABOUT A WEEK AFTER THE SEMINAR WHEN JON OUTCALT EMAILED ME PERSONALLY THAT HE HAD MADE A MULTI-MILLION DOLLAR SALE, THE <u>FIRST DAY</u>, BY USING MY METHODOLOGY. THE BUYER WAS A BULL AND WROTE A VERY LARGE CHECK, THAT VERY FIRST DAY.

I WAS TOLD IT WAS THE FIRST TIME THIS HAD EVER HAPPENED IN THEIR COMPANY.

YOU MIGHT ASK, "WHY DID THE BUYER DO THAT?" THE ANSWER IS BECAUSE, 1) "HE WANTED TO GET THE PROCESS GOING," 2) "DIDN'T WANT TO WASTE HIS OWN TIME," AND 3) THE "SUBJECT TO" AGREEMENT MADE IT A NON-RISK SITUATION. IF HE DIDN'T LIKE THE SPECIFICS, DETAILS, AND INGREDIENTS OF THE CONTRACT TO FOLLOW, AND DIDN'T AGREE WITH THE BOTTOM-LINE PRICE, THE COMPANY WAS <u>LEGALLY BOUND</u> TO REFUND HIS DEPOSIT AND HAVE THE CONTRACT "NULL AND VOID."

© 2021 Charles J. Clarke III. "Bulls, Owls, Lambs and Tigers®" is a registered federal trademark of Charles J. Clarke III since 1988. Personality Selling™ and BOLT™ are Trademarks of Charles J. Clarke III. NO reproduction in any form is allowed.

# Bulls, Owls, Lambs and Tigers®: Personality Selling™

THIS IS HOW COMPANIES THAT SELL CUSTOMIZED PRODUCT CAN ASK THE QUESTION, "WHAT DO YOU THINK ABOUT GOING AHEAD WITH THIS TODAY?" AND GET A SALE THE <u>FIRST DAY</u>.

OBVIOUSLY, NOT EVERY CUSTOMER WANTS TO BUY THE FIRST DAY, BUT SOME DO. AT LEAST GIVE THOSE THAT <u>WANT TO,</u> "GET ER DONE!" (LARRY THE CABLE GUY) "A <u>CHANCE</u>" TO GET IT STARTED.

THE ABOVE IS NOT PRESSURING THE POTENTIAL BUYER, IF BUYING THE FIRST DAY IS WHAT THEY WANT TO DO, AFTER THEY ARE SHOWN OPTIONS IN DOING SO.

**AT LEAST GIVE THEM THE OPPORTUNITY.**

**DOING LONG WRITTEN PROPOSALS**

IF YOU ARE IN THE BUSINESS OF WRITING LONG, WRITTEN PROPOSALS, YOU KNOW THEY ARE USUALLY WRITTEN IN "SEQUENTIAL ORDER," ENDING WITH THE PRICE.

WHAT DO BULL BUYERS <u>USUALLY</u> DO WHEN HANDED THIS **LONG PROPOSAL**? THEY IMMEDIATELY TURN TO THE LAST PAGE, OR THE PAGE THAT HAS THE PRICE. SO, I ASK YOU, IF YOU KNOW THE PERSON IS A BULL, WHY WOULDN'T YOU PUT THE PRICE ON THE <u>FIRST</u> PAGE, OR AT LEAST <u>ONE OF</u> THE FIRST PAGES?

JUST SOMETHING FOR YOU TO THINK ABOUT!

# NOTES

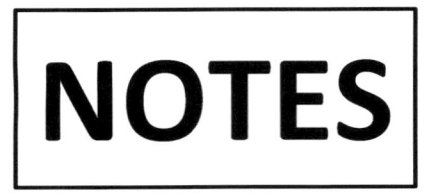

THINGS I AGREE WITH

THINGS I DISAGREE WITH

THINGS I NEED TO WORK ON

ACTION PLAN FOR ME

# CHAPTER 10

> # LIE/MYTH #7: IF PEOPLE ARE MARRIED, THEY WOULD <u>NOT</u> BUY IF THEIR SPOUSE IS NOT THERE, IF IT IS SOMETHING THAT WOULD INVOLVE THE SPOUSE.

SOME OF THE "ARGUMENTS" THAT SALESPEOPLE SAY WHEN THEY AGREE WITH THIS MYTH, ARE:

1) IF I WOULD BUY THIS ITEM WITHOUT MY SPOUSE'S APPROVAL, MY SPOUSE WOULD WANT TO DIVORCE ME.

THAT'S WHY I SUGGEST (IF NEEDED) TO WRITE THE CONTRACT (PURCHASE AGREEMENT), "SUBJECT TO SPOUSE'S APPROVAL."

> **BULLS AND TIGERS (MALE AND FEMALE) SAY THEY WOULD HAVE <u>NO</u> PROBLEM SIGNING A CONTRACT ON A HOME, FURNITURE, OR SOMETHING THAT WOULD INVOLVE THEIR SPOUSE, WITHOUT THEIR SPOUSE BEING THERE (AND REMAIN MARRIED).**

> **OWL AND LAMB BUYERS HAVE A HIGHER PROBABILITY OF <u>NOT</u> DOING THIS.**

# Bulls, Owls, Lambs and Tigers®: Personality Selling™

ON A PRODUCT THAT MIGHT INVOLVE BOTH SPOUSES, HERE IS WHAT I'M SUGGESTING. IF <u>YOU</u> WOULD NOT BUY WITHOUT YOUR SPOUSE BEING THERE, EVEN WITH A "SUBJECT TO SPOUSE'S APPROVAL," THEN <u>YOU</u> PROBABLY HAVE THE "VOODOO WHAMMY" IN YOUR SUBCONSCIOUS BRAIN. YOU WOULD HAVE A HIGHER PROBABILITY OF <u>NOT WANTING TO ASK,</u> "WHAT DO YOU THINK ABOUT GOING AHEAD WITH THIS TODAY?" TO SOMEONE WHOSE SPOUSE IS NOT THERE.

I SAY, "GET OVER IT," AND ASK ANYWAY!

### EXAMPLE OF GENERAL NORMAN SCHWARZKOPF

### (WHO HAS SINCE PASSED AWAY):

A NUMBER OF YEARS AGO I WAS TOLD BY A CUSTOM BUILDER IN A POLO GATED COMMUNITY IN TAMPA, FLORIDA, THAT GENERAL NORMAN SCHWARZKOPF BOUGHT A MULTI-MILLION DOLLAR HOME FROM THEM, ON THE VERY FIRST DAY.

THE CUSTOM BUILDER'S SALESPERSON HAD JUST BEEN THROUGH MY 3-DAY "MASTER CLOSER TRILOGY™" AND SHE ASKED THE "FIVE MAGIC QUESTIONS™." AFTER QUESTION #5, THE GENERAL SAID, "YES." HIS WIFE WAS NOT THERE AND THERE WAS <u>NO,</u> "SUBJECT TO WIFE'S APPROVAL." THE SALES LADY WAS "BLOWN AWAY" THAT THE GENERAL SAID, "YES!" NO ONE HAD EVER BOUGHT FROM HER THE FIRST DAY IN THIS MULTI-MILLION DOLLAR COMMUNITY, MUCH LESS WITHOUT THEIR SPOUSE BEING THERE. ("TRUE/TRUE" STORY) TIGER "TRUTH CODE" FOR "IT REALLY HAPPENED" (PROMISE/PROMISE)

YOUR THOUGHTS?

## EXAMPLE FROM AUTOMOBILE SALES

I HEAR THIS EXAMPLE QUITE FREQUENTLY FROM WOMEN. "I WAS TRYING TO BUY A CAR, AND AFTER I HAD CHOSEN THE CAR I WANTED, THE SALESPERSON SAID, "I NOTICED FROM YOUR LEFT HAND THAT YOU ARE WEARING A WEDDING RING. LET ME SUGGEST THAT BEFORE WE GO ANY FURTHER, WHY DON'T YOU BRING IN YOUR HUSBAND?"

IF YOU ARE A WOMAN, HAVE YOU EVER HEARD SOMETHING SIMILAR TO THAT? LET ME KNOW YOUR STORIES.

---

ON THAT LAST EXAMPLE, NEEDLESS TO SAY, THAT WOULD BE A "FIVE BOMBS" ON A FIVE-TO-ONE "TORTURE SCALE" (FOR THE BUYER AND FOR THE SALESPERSON, **AFTER SHE UNLOADED ON HIM).**

# NOTES

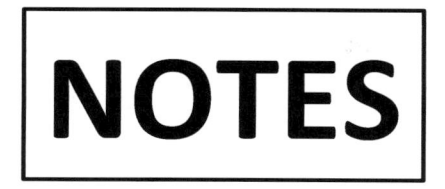

THINGS I AGREE WITH

THINGS I DISAGREE WITH

THINGS I NEED TO WORK ON

ACTION PLAN FOR ME

# CHAPTER 11

> # LIE/MYTH #8: CROSSED ARMS AND NO SMILE MEANS A PERSON IS DEFENSIVE.

CROSS YOUR ARMS IN FRONT OF YOU RIGHT NOW. TAKE THE SMILE OFF YOUR FACE. LOOK IN THE MIRROR. WHAT DOES IT LOOK LIKE TO YOU? IF YOU ARE A BULL, YOU ARE NOT GOING TO TAKE ME UP ON LOOKING IN THE MIRROR, BECAUSE YOU KNOW IT IS WHAT **YOU** DO, AND IT IS COMFORTABLE.

> # THAT STANCE OF CROSSED ARMS, WITH NO SMILE, ("BULL BODY LANGUAGE") ACTUALLY IS A <u>"BUYING SIGN"</u> FOR THE BULL MAN & BULL WOMAN.

THIS TIGHT BODY LANGUAGE POSITION (ARMS CROSSED) HAS BEEN WRITTEN ABOUT IN OTHER BOOKS AND HAS BEEN SPOKEN ABOUT IN SEMINARS, AS BEING NEGATIVE.

BULLS WILL TELL YOU THAT IT IS A VERY <u>COMFORTABLE</u>, <u>NATURAL</u> POSITION AND IT MEANS THEY ARE PAYING ATTENTION (A BUYING SIGN/NOT DEFENSIVE).

I RECENTLY SAW A SEGMENT OF BILL O'RILEY'S, "THE NO-SPIN ZONE," AND HE HAD ON A SO-CALLED, "BODY LANGUAGE EXPERT," WHO WAS ANALYZING A CLIP OF A WELL-KNOWN BULL LADY IN HER "BULL STANCE." THIS "EXPERT" POINTED OUT HOW THE WOMAN'S BODY LANGUAGE MEANT SHE WAS BEING COMPLETELY DEFENSIVE. NOT SO! SHE WAS JUST BEING A CONTENT BULL.

"MISREADING" A PERSON'S BODY LANGUAGE CAN EQUATE TO LOSING A SALE.

> WHEN LAMBS AND OWLS CROSS THEIR ARMS, IT COULD, INDEED, BE A DEFENSIVE STANCE. CROSSED ARMS COULD ALSO MEAN THE PERSON IS COLD.

## QUICK CLIP-MORE ON BODY LANGUAGE

## OWLS PERCH WITH NO SMILE

PUT YOUR HAND ON YOUR CHIN AND YOUR OTHER ARM UNDER THE ELBOW OF THE HAND ON YOUR CHIN. COME ON, PERCH! THAT'S WHAT OWLS DO. IF YOU DID IT NATURALLY, YOU'RE PROBABLY AN OWL.

## LAMBS "HEAD-BOB" WITH AN AGREEABLE SMILE.

YOU CAN ASK A LAMB A QUESTION THEY DISAGREE WITH AND THEY WILL SAY "NO," BUT THEIR HEAD IS STILL SAYING "YES" TO YOU, WITH A HEAD-BOB, BUT IT MEANS "NO." THIS CONFUSES BULLS, BUT LAMBS KNOW WHAT I MEAN.

## TIGERS TALK A LOT WITH THEIR HANDS, AND JUST PLAIN TALK A LOT, AND ARE VERY ANIMATED, LIKE CARTOON CHARACTERS.

TIGERS ALSO MOVE AROUND A LOT IF THEY ARE STANDING UP. I CALL IT THE "TIGER DANCE." THEY JUST CONSTANTLY HAVE A STRONG ENERGY URRENT GOING THROUGH THEM AND ARE HIGHLY EMOTIONAL.

IT'S ALL GOOD! *IT'S JUST ALL DIFFERENT.*

## BECOME A REAL BODY LANGUAGE EXPERT IN BOLT™.

# NOTES

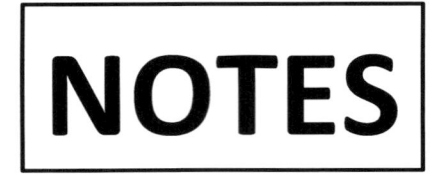

THINGS I AGREE WITH

THINGS I DISAGREE WITH

THINGS I NEED TO WORK ON

ACTION PLAN FOR ME

# CHAPTER 12

> # LIE/MYTH #9: IT IS VERY IMPORTANT THAT THE SALESPERSON TAKE CONTROL AND MAINTAIN CONTROL THROUGHOUT THE SALES PROCESS, AND THAT THE BUYER IS TOTALLY AWARE THAT THE SALESPERSON IS IN CONTROL.

**WHY IS THE ABOVE SO IMPORTANT TO SOME SALESPEOPLE?**

THIS ONE IS INTERESTING, BECAUSE OFTENTIMES IT COMES DOWN TO A "BULL FIGHT," WITH THE BULL SALESPERSON AND THE BULL BUYER; EACH ONE WANTING TO BELIEVE THEY ARE THE ONE IN CONTROL AND WANTING CONTROL.

BULL SALESPEOPLE OFTEN PUT "YES" TO THE QUESTION, BUT I AM SUGGESTING THAT THE ANSWER IS, "NO."

IF THE BULL BUYER BELIEVES THAT YOU ARE TRYING TO CONTROL THE SITUATION AND YOU MAKE THEM AWARE OF THAT, THE BULL BUYER WILL HIGHLY RESENT THAT AND OFTENTIMES WILL ACTUALLY WALK OUT ON YOU (LEAVE).

YOU ALWAYS WANT THE BULL BUYER TO BELIEVE THAT "THEY" ARE THE ONE IN CONTROL.

**WHAT IS WRONG WITH THEM ACTUALLY BEING IN CONTROL AND MAKING YOU THE SALE?**

YOUR THOUGHTS?

# Bulls, Owls, Lambs and Tigers®: Personality Selling™

ONE OF MY PHRASES I RECOMMEND USING AFTER THE QUALIFYING PROCESS IS, "HOW WOULD YOU LIKE TO PROCEED?" BULL OWNERS AND SALES MANAGERS HATE IT WHEN I RECOMMEND THAT, BECAUSE THEY SAY WE SHOULD NEVER LET THE BUYER PROCEED THE WAY THEY WANT TO. BUT, RATHER, WE SHOULD PROCEED THE WAY WE WANT TO PROCEED. SURE, DO THAT AND LOSE THE BULL! AFTER QUALIFYING, I RECOMMEND YOU SAY,

---

## "HOW WOULD YOU LIKE TO PROCEED?"

**THIS IS RECOMMENDED NO MATTER WHAT YOU ARE SELLING.**

---

**EXAMPLE OF SELLING IN AN EXPENSIVE GOLF COURSE RESORT COMMUNITY IN CALIFORNIA**

AFTER THE QUALIFYING PROCESS, SAY, "WE COULD NEXT:"

A) "SEE THE MODEL." (IF YOU HAVE ONE)
B) "GO AND LOOK AT A HOME PLAN UNDER CONSTRUCTION YOU DESCRIBED AND FOUND ON THE WEB SITE."
C) "DESCRIBE MORE OF THE FLOOR PLANS WE HAVE."
D) "ANSWER SOME OF YOUR QUESTIONS," OR
E) "TELL YOU MORE ABOUT OUR BUILDER AND OUR BUILDER'S STORY."

THEN, YOU WOULD SAY AGAIN, "HOW WOULD YOU LIKE TO PROCEED?"

WHEN YOU DO THIS, WHAT DO YOU THINK THE PROBABILITY IS THAT 90%+ CHOOSE TO SEE THE MODEL NEXT?

---

**IF YOU ASK THEM HOW THEY WANT TO PROCEED, LESS THAN 50% WANT TO SEE THE MODEL NEXT.**

---

ASK THEM, DON'T JUST TELL THEM! MODELS ARE OFTEN JUST "FLY PAPER" TO ATTRACT BUYERS IN.

---

© 2021 Charles J. Clarke III. "Bulls, Owls, Lambs and Tigers®" is a registered federal trademark of Charles J. Clarke III since 1988. Personality Selling™ and BOLT™ are Trademarks of Charles J. Clarke III. NO reproduction in any form is allowed.

# Bulls, Owls, Lambs and Tigers®: Personality Selling™

I KNOW THAT MAY SURPRISE SOME OF YOU, BUT LET'S LOOK AT OUR RESULTS.

### BULLS

BULLS HAVE A HIGHER PROBABILITY OF SAYING "LET'S GO LOOK AT THE ACTUAL HOME AND HOME SITE I COULD BUY," AND OFTEN WILL BUY THAT PARTICULAR HOME WITHOUT EVEN WANTING TO SEE THE MODEL (ESPECIALLY IF THE MODEL IS NOT THE FLOOR PLAN IN WHICH THEY ARE INTERESTED.)

### OWLS

OWLS HAVE A HIGHER PROBABILITY OF CHOOSING C & D, WANTING TO KNOW MORE ABOUT YOUR FLOOR PLANS (EVEN THOUGH THEY ALREADY SAW THEM ONLINE). THEY ALSO USUALLY HAVE A LIST OF QUESTIONS TO HAVE ANSWERED BEFORE THEY SEE THE MODEL. OWLS HAVE A HIGHER PROBABILITY OF CHOOSING THIS ORDER: C, D, E, A, B (FLOOR PLAN, QUESTIONS, BUILDER'S STORY, MODEL, SEEING WHAT IS AVAILABLE, THEN THE MODEL).

### LAMBS

LAMBS WILL PROCEED HOW YOU WANT TO, BUT THEIR PREFERENCE IS SIMILAR TO THE ORDER OF THE OWL.

### TIGERS

TIGERS HAVE A HIGHER PROBABILITY OF MAKING THE QUALIFYING PROCESS AS SHORT AS POSSIBLE, AND THEY USUALLY CHOOSE TO SEE THE MODEL NEXT (ABOUT A 95% PROBABILITY*).

TIGER SALESPEOPLE, WHO WOULD THEMSELVES ALWAYS WANT TO SEE THE MODEL RIGHT AWAY, ASSUME THAT <u>EVERYONE</u> WANTS TO DO THE SAME AS THEMSELVES. THEY JUST START OFF, AFTER <u>BRIEFLY</u> QUALIFYING TO SHOW THE MODEL, PROCEEDING THE WAY <u>THEY</u> WOULD WANT TO PROCEED.

YOU NOTICE THAT THROUGHOUT THE BOOK I USE THE REFERENCE TO "PROBABILITY." BULLS, OWLS, LAMBS & TIGERS® IS <u>NOT</u> 100% ACCURATE, BUT IT HAS A "PROBABILITY" OF BEING ABOUT 90%+ ACCURATE. WOULDN'T YOU LOVE TO HAVE 90%+ "PROBABILITY" OF WINNING IN LAS VEGAS OR ANY CASINO? THIS SYSTEM GIVES YOU THAT INEVITABLE "PROBABILITY" OF YOU BEING RIGHT AND BECOMING THE "MASTER CLOSER" (THE BEST OF THE BEST IN YOUR INDUSTRY).

---

**LET'S RETURN TO THE SALESPERSON <u>CONTROLLING</u> THE SALE.**

---

© 2021 Charles J. Clarke III. "Bulls, Owls, Lambs and Tigers®" is a registered federal trademark of Charles J. Clarke III since 1988. Personality Selling™ and BOLT™ are Trademarks of Charles J. Clarke III. NO reproduction in any form is allowed.

**Bulls, Owls, Lambs and Tigers®: Personality Selling™**

WHEN A SALESPERSON TRIES TO <u>CONTROL</u> THE SALE WITH A BULL AND TRIES TO <u>TELL</u> THE BULL HOW <u>THEY</u> (THE BULL) IS GOING TO PROCEED, IT COULD RESULT IN A <u>LOST SALE</u>, AND A "FIVE-BOMB EXPLOSION" ON THE "TORTURE SCALE" FOR BOTH THE BUYER AND THE SALESPERSON.

---

**AGAIN:**

"WE OFTEN SELL THE WAY WE WOULD LIKE TO BE SOLD AND THUS LOSE ½ TO ¾'S OF OUR POTENTIAL SALES."

**CHARLES CLARKE III**

# NOTES

THINGS I AGREE WITH

THINGS I DISAGREE WITH

THINGS I NEED TO WORK ON

ACTION PLAN FOR ME

# CHAPTER 13

## LIE/MYTH #10: IT IS VERY IMPORTANT TO STATE, RESTATE, AND VERIFY WHAT THE BUYER JUST SAID.

## SURE! DO THAT IF YOU COMPLETELY WANT TO LOSE THE BULL AND MAKE THE BULL AND OTHERS THINK YOU ARE AN IDIOT!

OWLS ARE THE ONLY PERSONALITY THAT LIKE THIS. TIGERS MIGHT **NEED** THIS, BUT THEY ARE NOT LISTENING.

LAST YEAR I WAS WITH A LARGE COMPANY IN SOUTH FLORIDA WHO HAD BROUGHT IN A CONSULTANT WHO RECOMMENDED DOING THE ABOVE MYTH. WHEN WE DID MYSTERY SHOPPING OF THIS COMPANY, BEFORE I DID MY THREE-DAY MASTER CLOSER SERIES WITH THEM, THIS IS WHAT WE FOUND.

(OUR MYSTERY SHOPPER WITNESSED THIS WITH A REAL BUYER.)

AFTER GREETING, THE BUYER ASKED FOR A BROCHURE AND A PRICE SHEET.

THE SALESPERSON, WHO HAD BEEN INSTRUCTED TO DO SO BY THE CONSULTANT, SAID, "SO YOU ARE SAYING YOU WANT A BROCHURE, IS THAT RIGHT?"

BUYER SAID, "YES! THAT'S WHAT I SAID."

SALESPERSON SAID, "AND YOU ALSO WANT A PRICE SHEET?"

BUYER SAID, "YES! THAT'S WHAT I SAID."

SALESPERSON SAID, "AND YOU WANT A PRICE SHEET, BECAUSE?"

BUYER SAID, "SO I KNOW THE PRICE."

SALESPERSON SAID, "SO THAT MEANS YOU HAVE A POSSIBLE INTEREST IN BUYING?"

BUYER SAID, "I WOULDN'T BE HERE IF I DIDN'T."

# Bulls, Owls, Lambs and Tigers®: Personality Selling™

IF YOU ARE STILL READING THIS, IT IS "LAUGHABLE" AND VERY SAD. IT IS A "TRUE-TRUE" STORY THAT OCCURRED.

IT CONTINUED ON LIKE THIS, EVEN IN THE DEMONSTRATION IN A VERY ELABORATE SALES DESIGN CENTER. OUR MYSTERY SHOPPER WITNESSED THAT ABOUT 20 MINUTES INTO THE DESIGN CENTER DEMONSTRATION, WITH ALL THIS STATING, RESTATING AND VERIFYING, THE POTENTIAL BUYER ACTUALLY SAID, "IS THIS A JOKE? ARE WE BEING TAPED? AM I GOING TO BE ON YOU TUBE?" AFTER THAT HE ACTUALLY WALKED OUT.

PLEASE DON'T DO THAT!

BULLS AND OTHERS DON'T LIKE, AND RESENT, ANYTHING BEING STATED, RESTATED AND VERIFIED. ONLY AN OWL WOULD ALLOW THAT WITH NO RESENTMENT.

YOUR THOUGHTS?

**THE ABOVE EXAMPLE WOULD ONLY BE ABOUT A TWO ON THE FIVE-TO-ONE "TORTURE SCALE."**

HOWEVER, WHY WOULD YOU WANT TO "TORTURE" YOUR BUYERS, EVEN A LITTLE BIT?

# NOTES

THINGS I AGREE WITH




THINGS I DISAGREE WITH




THINGS I NEED TO WORK ON




ACTION PLAN FOR ME

# Bulls, Owls, Lambs and Tigers®: Personality Selling™

## CHAPTER 14

> # LIE/MYTH #11: IF A BUYER ASKS FOR THE PRICE RIGHT AWAY, THE SALESPERSON SHOULD AVOID TELLING THEM THE PRICE RIGHT AWAY AND STAY ON COURSE.

YOU'VE READ BOOKS BEFORE IN SELLING THAT STATE THIS MYTH AND MANY REALLY BELIEVE IT.

I'M SUGGESTING THAT WHEN A POTENTIAL BUYER ASKS WHAT THE PRICE IS, NO MATTER WHAT THEIR PERSONALITY, GIVE IT TO THEM RIGHT AWAY. THAT'S WHAT THEY WANT! GIVE IT TO THEM.

ON A RECENT MYSTERY SHOP OF OURS, WE HAD THE MYSTERY SHOPPER ASK IN THE SHOWROOM "WHAT IS THE PRICE OF THIS AUTOMOBILE, AS IS?" (THERE WAS NO STICKER PRICE.)"

THE SALESPERSON SAID, "WELL, WE CAN GET TO THAT LATER. THE PRICE WOULDN'T MEAN ANYTHING TO YOU NOW, IF YOU DON'T KNOW ABOUT THE VALUE OF THE CAR AND WHAT EXTRAS IT HAS."

AFTER THE SALESPERSON FINISHED THEIR SENTENCE, OUR MYSTERY SHOPPER REPEATED, "WHAT IS THE PRICE OF THIS CAR?" (JUST LIKE A REAL-LIVE BULL BUYER WOULD DO.)

THE SALESPERSON REPEATED HER SENTENCE ABOUT VALUE AND TRIED TO PROCEED. OUR MYSTERY SHOPPER PROCEEDED WITH HIS REAL PERSONALITY AND SAID, "DO YOU 'KNOW' THE PRICE OF THIS AUTOMOBILE, AS IT IS?" SALESPERSON SAID, "YES." OUR MYSTERY SHOPPER SAID, "THEN TELL IT TO ME NOW!"

THE SALESPERSON THEN NERVOUSLY GAVE THE BASE PRICE OF THE CAR AND OUR BULL MYSTERY SHOPPER SAID, "IS THIS THE PRICE OF THIS CAR, AS IT IS, WITH ALL THE UPGRADES THAT ARE INCLUDED?"

THE SALESPERSON SAID, "NO, THE UPGRADES ARE ABOUT $8,000 MORE."

MYSTERY SHOPPER SAID, "THEN WHY DIDN'T YOU TELL ME THAT WHEN I ASKED THE PRICE OF THE CAR, AS IT IS?"

CAN YOU, THE READER, FEEL THE FRUSTRATION OF THE BUYER?

© 2021 Charles J. Clarke III. "Bulls, Owls, Lambs and Tigers®" is a registered federal trademark of Charles J. Clarke III since 1988. Personality Selling™ and BOLT™ are Trademarks of Charles J. Clarke III. NO reproduction in any form is allowed.

# Bulls, Owls, Lambs and Tigers®: Personality Selling™

WHY DO WE DO THIS TO OUR POTENTIAL BUYERS, IN ANY INDUSTRY?

WITH THIS AUTOMOBILE THERE WERE TWO PRICES, THE BASE PRICE AND THE PRICE OF THE AUTOMOBILE, "AS IS."

---

**LEGITIMATE ANSWER TO "WHAT IS THE PRICE OF THIS CAR?"**

**"THE PRICE OF THIS CAR, AS YOU SEE IT, IS $55,000, BUT THE BASE PRICE ON THIS CAR IS $47,000. IS THIS ABOUT THE PRICE YOU HAD IN MIND? WHAT PRICE RANGE DID YOU HAVE IN MIND WHEN YOU CAME IN?"**

---

IN MANY DIFFERENT INDUSTRIES, SALESPEOPLE ARE TAUGHT THE LIE AND MYTH THAT "IF A BUYER ASKS FOR THE PRICE TOO EARLY, WE SHOULD NOT GIVE THEM THE PRICE RIGHT AWAY. WE SHOULD TRY TO BUILD VALUE FIRST. "

---

**SURE, AND TORTURE THEM A "FIVE" ON A FIVE-TO-ONE "TORTURE SCALE."**

---

© 2021 Charles J. Clarke III. "Bulls, Owls, Lambs and Tigers®" is a registered federal trademark of Charles J. Clarke III since 1988. Personality Selling™ and BOLT™ are Trademarks of Charles J. Clarke III. NO reproduction in any form is allowed.

## Bulls, Owls, Lambs and Tigers®: Personality Selling™

I'M SUGGESTING THAT NO MATTER WHAT ANIMAL PERSONALITY YOU ARE WORKING WITH, YOU WANT TO DO THE FOLLOWING:

> **NO MATTER WHEN IT COMES UP, ANSWER THEIR QUESTIONS AND TELL THEM THE PRICE IF THEY ASK FOR IT. DON'T MAKE THEM ASK A SECOND TIME.**

GIVE THE POTENTIAL BUYER WHAT THEY WANT, WHEN THEY WANT IT!

**THIS REALLY IS "INTEGRITY SELLING!"**

YOUR THOUGHTS?

HOW ARE YOU GOING TO READ JUST YOUR OWN PRESENTATION?

> **BULLS & TIGERS HAVE A HIGHER PROBABILITY OF ASKING A DIRECT QUESTION ABOUT THE PRICE RIGHT AWAY, BUT SOMETIMES EVEN OWLS AND LAMBS ASK THIS, AND WANT TO KNOW THE ANSWER, WHEN THEY ASK IT.**

# NOTES

THINGS I AGREE WITH

THINGS I DISAGREE WITH

THINGS I NEED TO WORK ON

ACTION PLAN FOR ME

# CHAPTER 15

> # LIE/MYTH #12: IF A COUPLE IS MARRIED, THE WOMAN <u>ALWAYS</u> MAKES THE DECISION IN BUYING, IF IT APPLIES TO A HOME OR SOMETHING FOR THE HOME.

WHEN I GET TO THIS TOPIC IN MY SEMINARS AND COUNSELING, I GET A LOT OF DISAGREEMENT, BECAUSE IT IS SUCH AN INGRAINED MYTH. MOST MARRIAGES THAT ARE INTACT (GOOD MARRIAGES), BOTH THE MAN AND THE WOMAN ARE IN ON THE DECISION. FROM OUR RESEARCH OF ACTUAL BUYERS, IT APPEARS THAT WOMEN MAKE THAT DECISION NO MORE THAN 50% TO 60% OF THE TIME. IT'S CLOSER TO THE 50%.

IF THE MAN IS A TIGER OR BULL (THE TWO MORE ASSERTIVE ANIMAL PERSONALITIES), HE IS PROBABLY THE ONE MAKING THE DECISION, NOT HIS WIFE, IN BUYING THE HOME AND HOME FURNISHINGS.

YOUR THOUGHTS?

LIKE SO MANY OTHER LIES AND MYTHS IN SELLING, HERE'S WHAT I THINK HAPPENED OVER 50 YEARS AGO. SOME CONSULTANT STARTED BELIEVING AND SAYING THE WOMAN <u>ALWAYS</u> MAKES THE DECISIONS AS IT RELATES TO BUYING A HOME AND THE FURNISHINGS FOR A HOME, AND OTHER PEOPLE STARTED BELIEVING IT AND PASSED IT ON.

> **IT'S JUST NOT TRUE!**

CONSEQUENCES OF BELIEVING THIS: IF YOU REALLY BELIEVE THIS, YOU WILL GEAR YOUR PRESENTATION AND CLOSES TO THE WOMAN AND LOSE THE TIGER/BULL OR BULL/TIGER HUSBAND.

**Bulls, Owls, Lambs and Tigers®: Personality Selling™**

# SELL TO BOTH! NOT JUST THE WOMAN!

SEVERAL YEARS AGO, A NATIONAL BUILDER WHO WAS IN THE TOP 10 OF THE NATION'S LARGEST BUILDERS, TOOK THE IDEA TO HEART THAT THE WOMAN ALWAYS MAKES THE DECISION AND ACTUALLY CHANGED <u>ALL</u> THE STATIONERY TO PINK OR MAUVE TO CONNECT MORE WITH WOMEN. THIS REALLY HAPPENED (TRUE/TRUE.)

WELL, YOU CAN IMAGINE THE RESULTS. IT BACKFIRED ON THEM! BULL WOMEN FELT THEY WERE BEING PATRONIZED AND BULL MEN COULDN'T UNDERSTAND IT.

THE COLOR THAT IS LIKED THE LEAST BY BULLS IS PINK AND OTHER PASTEL COLORS. YES, OUR RESEARCH SHOWS THAT EACH OF THE ANIMAL PERSONALITIES HAS THEIR FAVORITE AND LEAST FAVORITE COLORS.

THIS BECOMES VERY IMPORTANT IN MERCHANDIZING AND PACKAGING, BUT IT IS NOT FOR NOW. IT IS A SUBJECT THAT IS COVERED IN DETAIL IN ANOTHER BOOK.

BE CAREFUL <u>NOT</u> TO GET SUCKED INTO THIS PAST AND CURRENT MYTH. IT CAN AFFECT YOUR SUCCESS IN A NEGATIVE WAY.

<u>PACKAGING</u>

JUST FOR YOUR EDIFICATION, THE FAVORITE COLORS OF EACH OF THE ANIMAL PERSONALITIES ARE

| | |
|---|---|
| **BULLS** | BLACK, DARK BROWN, DARK GREEN (HUNTER'S GREEN) |
| **OWLS** | GREY, BEIGE (THE EXCITING COLOR OF BEIGE) (THAT'S OWL HUMOR) |
| **LAMBS** | PASTELS-LIGHT BLUE, LIGHT YELLOW, LIGHT GREEN AND PINK (WHICH IS MORE GENDER-BASED) |
| **TIGERS** | RED, ORANGE, PURPLE, JEWEL TONES, AND PRIMARY COLORS |

HOW DOES THIS LINE UP WITH <u>YOUR OWN</u> PERSONALITY?

REMEMBER THESE ARE "PROBABILITY STATEMENTS" WITH 30+ YEARS OF OUR RESEARCH.

© 2021 Charles J. Clarke III. "Bulls, Owls, Lambs and Tigers®" is a registered federal trademark of Charles J. Clarke III since 1988. Personality Selling™ and BOLT™ are Trademarks of Charles J. Clarke III. NO reproduction in any form is allowed.

# NOTES

THINGS I AGREE WITH

THINGS I DISAGREE WITH

THINGS I NEED TO WORK ON

ACTION PLAN FOR ME

# CHAPTER 16

> # LIE/MYTH #13: EVEN IF THERE IS <u>NOT</u> AN URGENT SITUATION, THE SALESPERSON NEEDS TO CREATE "URGENCY" IN ORDER TO MOTIVATE THE BUYER.

THE ABOVE STATEMENT IS SO <u>UNTRUE</u> AND IS A VERY DETRIMENTAL MIND-SET.

I HEAR FROM COMPANIES ALL THE TIME WHEN I FIRST START WORKING WITH THEM, "PLEASE HELP OUR SALESPEOPLE FIND THE <u>URGENCY</u> FOR A BUYER 'GOING AHEAD WITH THIS TODAY.'"

> **APPROXIMATELY ½ OF THE POPULATION (LAMBS & OWLS) ARE REALLY "TURNED OFF" AND WILL NOT BUY WITH URGENCY CLOSES AND "TAKE-AWAY" CLOSES.**

### SELLING ROLEX WATCHES

**TAKE-AWAY CLOSE** – (TAKING IT AWAY FROM THEM) "MAYBE THIS PARTICULAR ROLEX IS <u>NOT</u> FOR YOU. MAYBE YOU SHOULD LOOK AT A LESS EXPENSIVE WATCH." THAT WOULD BE A MOTIVATOR FOR TIGERS AND BULLS AND A "DE-MOTIVATOR" FOR LAMBS AND OWLS.

### SELLING EXPENSIVE SUNGLASSES

**URGENCY CLOSE** – (APPLYING URGENCY SO THAT IF THE POTENTIAL BUYER DOES NOT BUY TODAY, THEY WILL LOSE OUT ON SOMETHING) SUCH AS "THE PRICE IS GOING UP," "OUR DISCOUNT IS ONLY GOOD TODAY," (IF THAT IS TRUE) "THIS IS OUR LAST PAIR OF THIS PARTICULAR STYLE." (IF THAT IS TRUE) THIS URGENCY CLOSE <u>"INCREASES"</u> THE PROBABILITY OF THE BULL/TIGER BUYING TODAY AND WOULD "DECREASE" THE PROBABILITY OF THE LAMB/OWL BUYING IT <u>AT ALL.</u>

# Bulls, Owls, Lambs and Tigers®: Personality Selling™

## SELLING EXPENSIVE CONDOMINIUM HOMES IN MANHATTAN

"SOMEONE ELSE IS LOOKING AT THIS SAME HOME. LET'S TAKE A LOOK AT YOUR SECOND FAVORITE, BECAUSE THIS ONE MIGHT BE GONE IF YOU DON'T BUY IT TODAY."

LAMBS AND OWLS (APPROXIMATELY 50% OF THE POPULATION) TELL US THAT ALL OF THE ABOVE URGENCY CLOSES ARE A "BIG TURN OFF" TO THEM AND WOULD MAKE THEM NOT EVEN COME BACK FOR THE APPOINTMENT THAT THE SALESPERSON FORCED UPON THEM. ASK LAMBS AND OWLS THAT YOU KNOW IF THIS IS TRUE. IT IS TRUE!

> IF YOU SAY TO A LAMB/OWL, "IF YOU DON'T BUY TODAY, IT MIGHT BE GONE TOMORROW" THE LAMB/OWL HAS A HIGH PROBABILITY OF SAYING SOMETHING LIKE, "QUE SERA SERA," OR "IF IT'S NOT MEANT TO BE" AND "IF IT'S NOT GOD'S WILL, IT MIGHT VERY WELL BE GONE TOMORROW," ADDING, "THAT WOULD BE OKAY WITH ME." YOU'VE HEARD THAT BEFORE, HAVEN'T YOU?

TIGERS AND BULLS ARE BIG ADVOCATES OF URGENCY CLOSES BECAUSE THEY WOULD AND DO WORK ON THEM.

> TIGERS AND BULLS RESPOND VERY WELL TO "FEAR OF LOSS." LAMBS AND OWLS DO NOT. LAMBS AND OWLS ARE NOT MOTIVATED BY LOSS BUT ARE MOTIVATED BY GAINS. RIGHT NOW YOU MIGHT NOT SEE A BIG DIFFERENCE BETWEEN THESE TWO. THE DIFFERENCE IS HUGE!

### EXAMPLE

A MAJOR UNIVERSITY CONDUCTED AN EXPERIMENT WITH MOTIVATING HIGH SCHOOL STUDENTS GOING ON TO COLLEGE. IT WAS A LONGITUDINAL EXPERIMENT INTO THE FUTURE, WHICH INVOLVED MANY FACETS.

WHAT STATEMENT BELOW DO YOU THINK WAS MORE MOTIVATIONAL?

A) IF YOU DO GET GOOD GRADES, YOU WILL BE ABLE TO GET INTO A GOOD COLLEGE! (KEY WORDS "DO" AND "WILL.")

OR

B) IF YOU DON'T GET GOOD GRADES, YOU WON'T BE ABLE TO GET INTO A GOOD COLLEGE! (KEY WORDS "DON'T" AND WON'T.")

# Bulls, Owls, Lambs and Tigers®: Personality Selling™

WRITE DOWN YOUR ANSWER OF WHICH DO YOU THINK WAS MORE MOTIVATIONAL TO THIS GROUP OF 1000 STUDENTS? WHICH MOTIVATES YOU MORE, A OR B?

THE ANSWER IS, IT WAS SPLIT ABOUT 50/50.

THE POINT IS ABOUT 50% OF PEOPLE ARE MORE MOTIVATED BY NON-URGENCY ("DO/WILL") AND ABOUT 50% ARE MOTIVATED BY URGENCY ("DON'T/WON'T").

BULLS AND TIGERS IN COLLEGE ARE MORE "PROCRASTINATORS." GIVEN A BIG ASSIGNMENT OF A MAJOR PAPER 15 WEEKS IN ADVANCE, WHEN DO TIGERS AND BULLS START WORKING ON IT? MANY TELL US, THE NIGHT BEFORE WITH AN ALL-NIGHTER AND DO A "DARN GOOD JOB OF IT!" I KNEW THIS TO BE TRUE WHEN I WAS A UNIVERSITY INSTRUCTOR AND COLLEGE PROFESSOR.

OWLS AND LAMBS TELL US THEY HAVE A HIGHER PROBABILITY OF WORKING ON IT ALL THROUGH THE SEMESTER AND HAVE IT COMPLETED WAY IN ADVANCE. HOW ABOUT YOU? HOW DOES THIS RELATE TO CLOSING AND URGENCY CLOSES?

> **TIGERS AND BULLS LIKE PRESSURE; LAMBS AND OWLS DON'T.**

> WE WILL SEE LATER FROM THE "LIE/MYTH #25 ON OBJECTIONS" THAT THERE ARE HUNDREDS OF OBJECTIONS THAT CAN BE BROKEN DOWN TO ONLY 7 OBJECTIONS.

LAMBS AND OWLS HAVE A HIGHER PROBABILITY OF SAYING, "I WANT TO THINK IT OVER." WHEN LAMBS SAY THIS, BULLS WANT TO APPLY URGENCY AND THUS LOSE THE SALE.

> **IS "I WANT TO THINK IT OVER" A REAL OBJECTION OR A SMOKE SCREEN? GO AHEAD AND ANSWER THAT.**

MORE BULLS AND SOME TIGERS SAY IT'S A "SMOKE SCREEN." I HEARD THE LATE (AND GREAT) ZIG ZIGLER SAY MANY TIMES IN HIS SEMINARS, "WHEN A BUYER SAYS THEY NEED TO THINK IT OVER, IT'S JUST A SMOKE SCREEN." THAT WAS ZIG ZIGLER, A TIGER/BULL, SAYING THAT.

I'M SUGGESTING THAT IF YOU REALLY THINK IT'S A SMOKE SCREEN YOU WILL TREAT IT AS A SMOKE SCREEN AND THUS LOSE THE LAMB. WITH THE LAMB (AND WITH THE OWL) IF YOU "BELIEVE" IT IS ONLY A SMOKE SCREEN YOU REALLY DON'T KNOW WHAT THEY ARE SAYING. BULLS SEE IT AS A SMOKE SCREEN, BECAUSE IF THEY SAID THAT (AND THEY WOULDN'T), IT WOULD BE A SMOKE SCREEN.

© 2021 Charles J. Clarke III. "Bulls, Owls, Lambs and Tigers®" is a registered federal trademark of Charles J. Clarke III since 1988. Personality Selling™ and BOLT™ are Trademarks of Charles J. Clarke III. NO reproduction in any form is allowed.

# Bulls, Owls, Lambs and Tigers®: Personality Selling™

> IN 1983 TOMMY HOPKINS AND I HAD A SERIES OF ABOUT THIRTEEN SEMINARS SCHEDULED ALL AROUND THE UNITED STATES. HE WROTE IN HIS BEST-SELLING BOOK, "MASTER THE ART OF CLOSING," MANY LISTS OF CLOSES, ONE OF WHICH IS THE "THINK IT OVER CLOSE."

YOU'LL PROBABLY RECOGNIZE A VARIATION OF IT. IT GOES SOMETHING LIKE THIS:

POTENTIAL BUYER SAYS, "I NEED TO THINK IT OVER."

**USING THAT LAST EXAMPLE OF THE EXPENSIVE CONDOMINIUM IN MANHATTAN**

THIS IS OFTEN AFTER POSSIBLY AN HOUR PLUS TOGETHER AND AFTER THE POTENTIAL BUYERS SAID THEY LOVED THE AREA, IT WAS DEFINITELY AN AREA THEY WANTED TO LIVE IN, THEY REALLY LIKED THAT PARTICULAR HOME, AND THEY COULD AFFORD IT.

HOWEVER, WHEN THE SALESPERSON SAID SOMETHING LIKE, "SO LET'S GO AHEAD WITH THIS TODAY," ONE OF THE POTENTIAL BUYERS SAID, "NO, I NEED TO THINK IT OVER."

DOES THIS SOUND FAMILIAR?

WHAT TOMMY HOPKINS TAUGHT AND WHAT OTHERS ADVOCATE TODAY, IS SAYING "WHAT DO YOU NEED TO THINK OVER?"

POTENTIAL LAMB BUYER RESPONSE, "EVERYTHING!"

SALESPERSON REPEATS AGAIN:

SALESPERSON: "WELL YOU SAID YOU LIKED THE AREA, THE HOME, THE SITE, AND THE PRICE. WHAT IS IT YOU NEED TO THINK OVER?"

AGAIN, THE ANSWER IS, "EVERYTHING. I JUST NEED TO THINK IT ALL OVER."

---

SALESPERSON CONTINUES

"IS IT THE HOME?" RESPONSE, "NO."

"IS IT THE AREA?" RESPONSE, "NO."

"IS IT THE PRICE?" RESPONSE, "NO."

"IS IT SOMETHING ABOUT ME?" RESPONSE, "NO."

"THEN WHAT IS IT?" RESPONSE, "I JUST NEED TO THINK IT ALL OVER."

**THE BULL SALESPERSON IS HIGHLY FRUSTRATED BECAUSE THEY WERE USING THE,"I'LL THINK IT OVER" CLOSE THAT NEVER WAS DESIGNED TO WORK ON LAMBS AND NEVER HAS!**

---

© 2021 Charles J. Clarke III. "Bulls, Owls, Lambs and Tigers®" is a registered federal trademark of Charles J. Clarke III since 1988. Personality Selling™ and BOLT™ are Trademarks of Charles J. Clarke III. NO reproduction in any form is allowed.

# Bulls, Owls, Lambs and Tigers®: Personality Selling™

> **IN MY OPINION IT IS A FRUSTRATING CLOSE THAT <u>NEVER</u> WORKED ON ANYONE AND HAS CAUSED MANY 1000'S OF SALES TO BE LOST!**

I CALL IT THE "IS IT THE"/"IS IT THE"/"IS IT THE" CLOSE AND IT BUGS EVERYONE. CAN YOU IMAGINE EVER DOING THAT WITH A BULL WHO SAID THEY JUST NEEDED TO THINK IT OVER TO GET ONE OTHER THING DONE? THE BULL WOULD WALK OUT AND THE LAMB WOULD NOT COME BACK FOR THE APPOINTMENT THAT THE BULL FORCED UPON THEM. LAMBS (AND OWLS) DON'T LIKE URGENCY AND "URGENCY CLOSES." PLEASE RE-READ THIS.

> "SO, WHAT SHOULD I DO IF A LAMB SAYS, 'I WANT TO THINK IT OVER'?"

IT'S OK TO ASK ONE TIME, "WHAT DO YOU WANT TO THINK OVER?" BUT STOP THERE IF THEY SAY, "EVERYTHING." (QUIT TORTURING PEOPLE)

> WRITE IT UP "SUBJECT TO THINKING IT OVER FOR 24 HOURS AND APPROVING OF THE CONDOMINIUM WITHIN 24 HOURS" AND DON'T BADGER THEM.

WRITE IT UP JUST LIKE YOU WOULD IF SOMEONE NEEDED TO BRING THEIR SPOUSE IN TO SEE IT TOMORROW, "SUBJECT TO SPOUSE COMING IN WITHIN 24 HOURS AND APPROVING OF HOME."

AT LEAST GIVE THEM THAT "OPPORTUNITY," "SUBJECT TO THINKING IT OVER."

IN EACH CASE, YOU COULD GET A CHECK AND A SIGNED CONTRACT.

IF YOU ARE A BULL SALESPERSON, A BULL SALES MANAGER, OR A BULL OWNER, I DON'T EXPECT YOU TO "GET THIS" OR UNDERSTAND THE REASONS FOR "SUBJECT TO THINKING IT OVER FOR 24 HOURS."

> **YOU DON'T HAVE TO "UNDERSTAND IT." JUST DO IT!**

> **IF YOU WANT, CONTACT ME PERSONALLY ABOUT THIS, FOR MORE EXPLANATION.**

THERE IS AN <u>"ART FORM"</u> TO CLOSE EACH OF THE FOUR ANIMAL PERSONALITIES AND THEIR SPOUSE, WHO IS OFTEN AN OPPOSITE PERSONALITY.

---

© 2021 Charles J. Clarke III. "Bulls, Owls, Lambs and Tigers®" is a registered federal trademark of Charles J. Clarke III since 1988. Personality Selling™ and BOLT™ are Trademarks of Charles J. Clarke III. NO reproduction in any form is allowed.

# Bulls, Owls, Lambs and Tigers®: Personality Selling™

SELLING IS AN ART AND A SCIENCE

**IF YOU USE URGENCY CLOSES ON THE 50% OF THE POPULATION THAT DOES NOT LIKE URGENCY CLOSES, IT'S A FIVE ON THE FIVE-TO-ONE "TORTURE SCALE" WITH THEM.**

DO YOU KNOW HOW TO SEAMLESSLY CLOSE EACH ANIMAL PERSONALITY?

I'M NOT TRYING TO BE COY IN NOT GIVING MORE INFORMATION ON THIS NOW, BUT IT IS REALISTIC THAT I CAN ONLY COVER SO MUCH IN THIS BOOK.

THE PURPOSE HERE IS TO GRAB YOUR ATTENTION IN CONVINCING YOU THAT YOU MAY BE CLOSING ONLY THE WAY <u>YOU</u> WOULD LIKE TO BE CLOSED, THUS LOSING APPROXIMATELY ½ OF YOUR POTENTIAL CLOSES. YOU HAVE TO PRACTICE, DRILL AND REHEARSE THIS. (PDR)

# NOTES

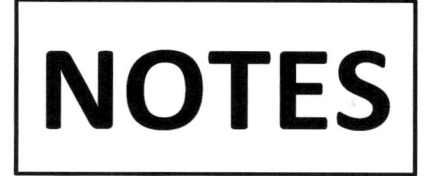

THINGS I AGREE WITH

THINGS I DISAGREE WITH

THINGS I NEED TO WORK ON

ACTION PLAN FOR ME

# CHAPTER 17

> # LIE/MYTH #14: MEN ARE ALWAYS MORE "LOGICAL" IN BUYING, WHILE WOMEN ARE ALWAYS MORE "EMOTIONAL."

NOT TRUE!

I THINK YOU PROBABLY SEE THE TREND NOW. BULLS, OWLS, LAMBS AND TIGERS® IS NOT "GENDER BASED" OR "GENDER BIASED." ABOUT 25% OF THE POPULATION IS EACH ANIMAL. THE SAME IS TRUE FOR MALENESS AND FEMALENESS, BEING ABOUT A 50%/50%, ON MOST ITEMS.

HAVE YOU READ OR HEARD OF THE FUN BOOK BY JOHN GRAY, "MEN ARE FROM MARS AND WOMEN ARE FROM VENUS?" THAT BOOK, WHICH I RECOMMEND, IS ABOUT ½ RIGHT, BUT IT IS FUN.

READ THAT AGAIN AND SEE IF YOU WOULD AGREE WITH THAT.

> **BULL WOMEN HAVE MORE IN COMMON, PERSONALITY-WISE, WITH BULL MEN, THAN THEY DO WITH LAMB WOMEN.**

> **TIGER WOMEN HAVE MORE IN COMMON, PERSONALITY-WISE, WITH TIGER MEN, THAN THEY DO WITH OWL WOMEN.**

READ JOHN GREY'S BOOK AND SEE IF YOU DISAGREE WITH ALL HIS PREMISES.

LAST YEAR AT A NATIONAL CONVENTION, I HAD TO LISTEN TO A FEMALE TIGER TALK ABOUT HER HUSBAND (WHO IS AN OWL), ON HOW DIFFERENT THEY WERE. HER CONCLUSION WAS WOMEN ARE MORE EMOTIONAL AND MEN ARE MORE LOGICAL AND THAT'S HOW WE SHOULD ALL TREAT MEN AND WOMEN (BASED SOLELY ON HER OWN EXPERIENCES). DON'T FALL INTO THAT TRAP! IF YOU HAVE FALLEN INTO THIS MYTH IN THE PAST, IT COULD HAVE AFFECTED YOUR SALES IN A NEGATIVE WAY (LOST SALES).

IF YOU TRY TO SELL A <u>NON-EMOTIONAL</u> BULL/OWL WOMAN WITH EMOTION, BECAUSE YOU BELIEVE THIS MYTH THEN SHE MIGHT TRY TO TAKE YOU TO THE "<u>SLAP YOU UP ROOM</u>" (IMAGINARY ROOM), WHERE SHE <u>REALLY WOULD LIKE TO TAKE YOU</u>!

# NOTES

THINGS I AGREE WITH

THINGS I DISAGREE WITH

THINGS I NEED TO WORK ON

ACTION PLAN FOR ME

# CHAPTER 18

## LIE/MYTH #15: THE KITCHEN AND MASTER BATHROOM ARE STILL THE MOST IMPORTANT ROOMS IN A NEW HOME.

**YOU CAN SEE THIS LIE/MYTH PRESENTED IN EVERY HUGE ANNUAL KITCHEN AND BATH SHOW. OF COURSE, IT IS SELF-SERVING FOR THEM. (AND THAT'S OK.)**

IT'S JUST NOT TRUE!

DO YOU WANT A QUICK REVIEW OF OUR 30 YEARS OF RESEARCH ON WHAT EACH ANIMAL SAYS IS THEIR FAVORITE ROOM?

GUESS THE FAVORITE ROOMS OR TYPE OF HOME EACH ANIMAL PERSONALITY PREFERS:

**BULL** _____

**OWL** _____

**LAMB** _____

**TIGER** _____

REMEMBER IT'S BASED ON "PROBABILITY."

**BULLS - THE DEN OR "ME" ROOM. BULLS ALSO PREFER THE FOYER- HALLWAY ENTRANCE- GRAND WITH HIGH CEILINGS.**

# Bulls, Owls, Lambs and Tigers®: Personality Selling™

BULLS ALSO PUT THE MOST EMPHASIS ON THE "ELEVATIONS OF THE HOME" OUTSIDE APPEARANCE. (DON'T REFER TO THE OUTSIDE APPEARANCE OF THE HOME AS AN <u>ELEVATION</u>-TOO MANY BUYERS (ESPECIALLY TIGERS) STILL THINK THAT MEANS THE NUMBER OF FEET ABOVE SEA LEVEL.)

---

**OWLS – IT'S THE OWL WHO PUTS THE MOST EMPHASIS ON THE KITCHEN AND ON THE PRACTICAL LIVING ROOM**

---

**LAMBS –THE WARM, COZY, FRIENDLY FAMILY ROOM**

WITH POSSIBLY A FIREPLACE. (YES, EVEN IN WARMER CLIMATES.)

---

**TIGERS – THE SENSUAL, SEXY MASTER BEDROOM WITH THE SENSUAL, SEXY MASTER BATH**

- (IN MORE EXPENSIVE HOMES THE <u>SITTING ROOM</u> OFF THE MASTER BEDROOM.)
- THE MASTER BATHROOM WITH AN "OOOH, BUBBA TUB." ("OOOH, BUBBA. LOOK AT THAT TUB!") THERE'S A LONG STORY ATTACHED TO THAT, BUT NOT FOR NOW.
- THE SAME BATHTUB THAT OWLS WOULD SAY IS "IMPRACTICAL," TIGERS LOVE.
- ENTERTAINMENT CENTERS

# Bulls, Owls, Lambs and Tigers®: Personality Selling™

## FEATURE BENEFIT SELLING

> "A FEATURE IS A FEATURE, BUT THE BENEFIT IS DIFFERENT FOR EACH ANIMAL PERSONALITY."
>
> **CHARLES CLARKE III**

NOT EVERYONE LIKES THE SAME THING OR THE SAME FEATURE.

---

**EXAMPLE**

OUT OF 100 FEATURES AND ATTRIBUTES WOULD YOU AGREE THAT OUT OF 2000 BUYERS, MOST EVERYONE PUTS ENERGY-EFFICIENCY, MOLD-PROOF AND FIRE-PROOF AT THE TOP 10%? HOW ABOUT THE TOP 25%?

---

IN A RANDOM TEST OF A GROUP OF ACTUAL POTENTIAL BUYERS, ONLY OWLS AND LAMBS HAD THESE THREE VARIABLES IN THE TOP 25%. TIGERS HAD THOSE THREE ITEMS IN THE LOWER 25% AND BULLS HAD THEM IN THE LOWER 50%.

---

THIS ACTUALLY "SHOCKS" SOME PEOPLE WHO SAY EVERYONE SHOULD BE INTERESTED IN ENERGY EFFICIENCY. YET TIGERS DO NOT PUT ENERGY EFFICIENCY IN THE TOP 75% OF FEATURES AND BENEFITS. OBVIOUSLY NOT EVERYONE LIKES THE SAME THING.

LET'S DO A COUPLE MORE. "WHAT IS THE FEATURE OF A HOME WITH A CEILING HEIGHT OF 20 FEET?" GO AHEAD AND ANSWER THAT. (IT'S KIND OF A TRICK QUESTION.)

# Bulls, Owls, Lambs and Tigers®: Personality Selling™

THE <u>FEATURE</u> IS THE 20 FT CEILING. THE BENEFIT IS DIFFERENT FOR EACH ANIMAL PERSONALITY.

---

**THE FEATURE OF A 20 FT CEILING FOR ANY OF THE ANIMAL PERSONALITIES IS THE 20 FT CEILING.**

**FOR THE <u>TIGER</u> THE BENEFIT IS: FUN, EXCITING AND DIFFERENT.**

**FOR THE <u>BULL</u> THE BENEFIT IS: STRIKING, IMPRESSIVE AND MAKES A STATEMENT.**

**FOR THE <u>OWL</u> AND <u>LAMB</u> IT IS ACTUALLY AN "ANTI-BENEFIT."**

> **THE <u>OWL</u> LIKES A HOME THAT IS PRACTICAL, EFFICIENT & FUNCTIONAL. TO THEM, A 20 FT CEILING IS NONE OF THOSE.**

> **A <u>LAMB</u> LIKES A HOME THAT IS WARM, COZY AND COMFORTABLE.**

---

## ASSIGNMENT – LIST 20 FEATURES AND THEN THE BENEFITS FOR EACH ANIMAL PERSONALITY, FOR <u>EACH</u> OF YOUR PRODUCT LINES.

WE HAVE 30 YEARS OF RESEARCH ON JUST ABOUT EVERY FEATURE IMAGINABLE FOR EVERY PRODUCT, AND WHAT EACH ANIMAL PERSONALITY SAYS IS THE VALUE TO THEM AND THEIR PERSONALITY.

**IT TRULY IS AN AMAZING SCIENCE!**

HERE IS THE MISTAKE THAT SALESPEOPLE CAN RUN INTO.

"I CAN HARDLY WAIT TO SHOW YOU THE "<u>FUN</u>" <u>FEATURE</u> OF THIS. IT IS FUN, EXCITING AND HUGELY SPACIOUS."

YOU SEE WHAT IS COMING. THEY MAY BE PRESENTING TO AN OWL, WHO WILL BE TOTALLY UNIMPRESSED AND THEY WILL DISCOUNT EVERYTHING ELSE THE SALESPERSON SAYS. THE OWL MAY SEE THE "FUN" FEATURES AS SUPERFLUOUS AND JUST WANT YOU TO TALK ABOUT THE PRACTICAL FEATURES.

---

© 2021 Charles J. Clarke III. "Bulls, Owls, Lambs and Tigers®" is a registered federal trademark of Charles J. Clarke III since 1988. Personality Selling™ and BOLT™ are Trademarks of Charles J. Clarke III. NO reproduction in any form is allowed.

# Bulls, Owls, Lambs and Tigers®: Personality Selling™

DO YOU HAVE FOUR DIFFERENT PRESENTATIONS (DEMONSTRATIONS); ONE FOR EACH PERSONALITY WITH FEATURE/BENEFIT DEMONSTRATIONS DESIGNED FOR EACH PERSONALITY?

WHATEVER THEY CHOOSE, YOU GIVE THEM THAT KIND OF PRESENTATION.

NO MATTER WHAT YOU ARE SELLING, YOUR PRODUCT HAS 4 DIFFERENT ATTRIBUTES. YOU ASK: WHAT DO YOU WANT IT TO ACCOMPLISH? DO YOU WANT IT TO BE:

A) STRIKING, IMPRESSIVE AND MAKE A STATEMENT, (BULL)
B) PRACTICAL, EFFICIENT AND FUNCTIONAL, (OWL)
C) WARM, COZY AND COMFORTABLE, (LAMB) OR
D) FUN, EXCITING AND DIFFERENT? (TIGER)

WHY WOULD YOU "TORTURE" YOUR BUYER EVEN A LITTLE BIT?

**NOT GIVING THE KIND OF PRESENTATION THEY WANT IS MEDIOCRE. IT'S A POSSIBLE THREE, ON THE FIVE-TO-ONE "TORTURE SCALE," BUT IT'S ALSO JUST VERY IRRITATING.**

© 2021 Charles J. Clarke III. "Bulls, Owls, Lambs and Tigers®" is a registered federal trademark of Charles J. Clarke III since 1988. Personality Selling™ and BOLT™ are Trademarks of Charles J. Clarke III. NO reproduction in any form is allowed.

# NOTES

THINGS I AGREE WITH

THINGS I DISAGREE WITH

THINGS I NEED TO WORK ON

ACTION PLAN FOR ME

# Bulls, Owls, Lambs and Tigers®: Personality Selling™

## CHAPTER 19

## LIE/MYTH #16: IT IS OF UTMOST IMPORTANCE TO FIND COMMON GROUND WITH THE BUYER AND MAINTAIN COMMON GROUND THROUGHOUT THE

THE BOTTOM LINE IS THAT THE TWO NON-EMOTIONAL PERSONALITIES, BULLS AND OWLS, DO <u>NOT</u> WANT YOU TO BUILD COMMON GROUND AND RESENT IT IF YOU DO. (50% OF THE POPULATION)

YOU BUILD "COMMON GROUND" WITH THE BULL AND THE OWL BY **NOT TRYING** TO BUILD COMMON GROUND WITH THEM. DOES THAT MAKE SENSE?

### EXAMPLE

### SELLING CELL PHONES

IN THE SPRING OR SUMMER, A BULL BUYER DRIVES INTO THE PARKING LOT OF A CELL PHONE BUSINESS. THE SALESPERSON NOTICES THE POTENTIAL BUYER GET OUT OF HIS CONVERTIBLE AND THE SALESPERSON NOTICES GOLF CLUBS STICKING OUT OF THE CAR.

AFTER ENTERING THE BUSINESS AND AFTER MEETING AND GREETING, THE POTENTIAL BUYER POINTS TO A PARTICULAR CELL PHONE AND ASKS THE PRICE OF THE PHONE.

**SALESPERSON:** "I COULDN'T HELP BUT NOTICE YOU HAVE GOLF CLUBS IN YOUR CAR. ARE YOU GOING TO BE PLAYING TODAY?"

**BULL BUYER:** "YES, WHAT IS THE PRICE OF THIS PARTICULAR CELL PHONE?"

**SALESPERSON:** "OH, WHERE WILL YOU BE PLAYING?"

**BULL BUYER:** "MEADOWVIEW, AND THE PRICE IS?"

# Bulls, Owls, Lambs and Tigers®: Personality Selling™

> **THE BULL-OWL DOES NOT WANT YOU TO BUILD COMMON GROUND AND YOU BUILD COMMON GROUND BY <u>NOT</u> TRYING TO BUILD COMMON GROUND.**

THE BULL/OWL IS NOT LOOKING FOR A "NEW FRIEND." THEY JUST WANT TO POSSIBLY <u>BUY</u> WHAT YOU ARE SELLING.

> **THIS IS A GOOD SOLID FOUR ON THE FIVE-TO-ONE "TORTURE SCALE" FOR "SOME" BUYERS.**

DOES THIS MAKE SENSE?

THIS FLIES IN THE FACE OF ALMOST EVERYTHING ELSE YOU HAVE HEARD OR READ ABOUT "<u>ALWAYS BUILD COMMON GROUND WITH EVERYONE!</u>"

# NOTES

THINGS I AGREE WITH

THINGS I DISAGREE WITH

THINGS I NEED TO WORK ON

ACTION PLAN FOR ME

# CHAPTER 20

## LIE/MYTH #17: MEMORIZING "SCRIPTS" WORD FOR WORD, AND USING THE MEMORIZED SCRIPT, WORD FOR WORD, IS EXTREMELY IMPORTANT FOR THE SALESPERSON TO BECOME THE ABSOLUTE BEST.

I COULDN'T DISAGREE WITH THIS MORE!

TWO REASONS I AM SO OPPOSED ARE #1) IT DOESN'T WORK IF SALESPEOPLE JUST MEMORIZE CLOSES WITHOUT KNOWING WHICH CLOSES WORK AND DON'T WORK WITH DIFFERENT PERSONALITIES, AND #2) SALESPEOPLE BECOME "ROBOTIC" AS A RESULT OF JUST MEMORIZING LISTS OF CLOSES.

MANY OF THESE LISTS OF CLOSES WERE DEVELOPED IN THE LATE 1950'S AND 1960'S BY J. DOUGLAS EDWARDS', (NOT THE NEWSCASTER) "FOUNDATIONS OF MODERN SELLING." HE WAS THE INSPIRATION BEHIND TOMMY HOPKINS. IT MAY HAVE BEEN RIGHT FOR THE 1950'S, 1960'S, AND POSSIBLY EVEN THE 1970'S AND 1980'S, BUT THE MATERIAL IS OUTDATED AND, IN MANY CASES, JUST PLAIN INACCURATE FOR THIS TIME PERIOD.

DURING OUR LAST RECENT RECESSION FOLLOWING THE "BOOM" OF '05 AND '06, MANY COMPANIES REVERTED BACK TO THESE INACCURATE, MEMORIZED SCRIPTS, WORD FOR WORD, AND SAW THEIR SALES PLUMMET EVEN MORE. THOSE WORD-FOR-WORD, MEMORIZED SCRIPTS MAKE A SALESPERSON NOT THINK AND NOT PAY ATTENTION TO THEIR BUYER (TWO THINGS THAT ARE EXTREMELY IMPORTANT IN BECOMING A MASTER CLOSER).

EARLIER I GAVE AN EXAMPLE UNDER MY "LIE/MYTH #13," ABOUT URGENT CLOSING THAT CAME DIRECTLY OUT OF J. DOUGLAS EDWARDS FROM THE 1950'S AND LATER ADOPTED BY TOMMY HOPKINS IN HIS, "MASTER THE ART OF SELLING."

TOMMY HOPKINS' BOOK IS STILL IN PRINT. GET A COPY AND SPECIFICALLY LOOK AT THE CLOSES. I HIGHLY RECOMMEND YOU READ THAT BOOK AND J. DOUGLAS EDWARDS' BOOK. THEY ARE BOTH CLASSICS. THAT WAY YOU WILL KNOW MORE FROM WHERE I AM COMING.

LET ME GIVE JUST TWO EXAMPLES OF CLOSES FROM THOSE WORKS.

# Bulls, Owls, Lambs and Tigers®: Personality Selling™

## 1) THE FEEL, FELT, FOUND CLOSE

### AND

## 2) THE "T-BAR"/BEN FRANKLIN CLOSE

**EXAMPLE 1**

**"FEEL, FELT, FOUND"**

THIS CLOSE CAN BE USED IN SEVERAL SITUATIONS, AND CAN BE USED WHEN A POTENTIAL BUYER SAYS, "THEY WANT A LOWER PRICE."

SALESPERSON IS SUPPOSED TO SAY, "I CAN APPRECIATE HOW YOU "<u>FEEL</u>," WE HAVE HAD OTHER BUYERS WHO HAVE "<u>FELT</u>" THAT WAY ALSO, AND THEY "<u>FOUND</u>" THAT IF WE LOWERED THE PRICE FOR THEM, THAT IT WOULD HURT THE OVERALL VALUE OF OUR PRODUCT.

CAN YOU SEE TO WHOM THAT COULD "POSSIBLY" APPEAL? THE ANSWER IS THE LAMB, BUT HOW DO YOU THINK THE BULL WOULD REACT TO THAT?

I GET SO SICK AND TIRED OF THIS PARTICULAR CLOSE BEING USED SO OFTEN, BECAUSE IT ONLY WORKS ON LESS THAN ¼ OF THE POPULATION, AND IT IS SO "TRANSPARENT."

**BULLS DON'T CARE ABOUT "FEEL, FELT, FOUND" AND RESENT YOU EVEN TALKING LIKE THAT TO THEM. THE BULL SAYS "I DON'T CARE HOW YOU OR OTHERS FEEL OR WHAT YOU FELT OR FOUND. JUST GIVE ME A LOWER PRICE AND QUIT TALKING DOWN TO ME!"**

# Bulls, Owls, Lambs and Tigers®: Personality Selling™

THAT IS AN EXACT QUOTE I HEARD FROM A PROSPECTIVE BULL BUYER BUYING <u>MEDICAL EQUIPMENT</u>, WHERE I OBSERVED THE SALESPERSON USING THE "FEEL, FELT, FOUND" CLOSE ON THE WRONG PERSONALITY.

> DON'T INSULT THE INTELLIGENCE OF THE BUYER, BY USING OUTDATED, ROBOTIC CLOSES THAT NEVER WORKED, WITH SOME PERSONALITIES.

> **EXAMPLE #2**

> **THE "T BAR CLOSE," ALSO KNOWN AS THE "BEN FRANKLIN CLOSE," HAS ALWAYS TO BE DONE SITTING DOWN AND IN WRITING TO BE EFFECTIVE WITH OWLS.**

AN <u>EXCELLENT</u> CLOSE, EVEN TO THIS DAY, BUT WHEN SALESPEOPLE ARE ASKED TO MEMORIZE THIS CLOSE, THEY ARE NOT TOLD THAT IT ONLY WORKS ON ABOUT ¼ OF ALL PEOPLE (OWLS).

> **IT IS AN OWL CLOSE THAT WORKS VERY WELL ON OWLS**

IN THE AUTO-BIOGRAPHY OF BEN FRANKLIN, BEN FRANKLIN EXPRESSED HOW HE MADE DECISIONS. WHEN HE HAD TO MAKE A DECISION, HE SAID HE WOULD WRITE DOWN ALL THE REASONS FOR GOING AHEAD WITH IT IN ONE COLUMN AND ALL THE REASONS FOR NOT GOING AHEAD WITH IT IN ANOTHER COLUMN. IN SOME CASES, HE "WEIGHTED" SOME OF HIS ANSWERS WITH MORE EMPHASIS. HE WOULD THEN METHODICALLY AND ANALYTICALLY MEASURE THE LOGICAL ANSWERS.

BEN FRANKLIN WAS AN OWL. (OWL WITH BULL TO OWL WITH TIGER, BUT AN OWL)

> MY POINT IS THAT THIS IS AN OWL CLOSE, TO BE USED ON OWLS ONLY! WITH OTHER PERSONALITIES IT JUST GETS THEM AGGRAVATED.
>
> IF YOU USE THE BEN FRANKLIN CLOSE WITH TIGERS, CAN'T YOU JUST IMAGINE THEM "WONDERING WHAT THEY ARE GOING TO HAVE FOR DINNER," AND NOT PAYING ANY ATTENTION TO ANYTHING THE SALESPERSON SAYS?

© 2021 Charles J. Clarke III. "Bulls, Owls, Lambs and Tigers®" is a registered federal trademark of Charles J. Clarke III since 1988. Personality Selling™ and BOLT™ are Trademarks of Charles J. Clarke III. NO reproduction in any form is allowed.

# Bulls, Owls, Lambs and Tigers®: Personality Selling™

THE "T BAR CLOSE" IS ACTUALLY THE SAME AS THE BEN FRANKLIN CLOSE.

ON THE ONE SIDE (LEFT) LIST ALL THE REASONS FOR GOING AHEAD. ON THE OTHER SIDE (RIGHT) LIST ALL THE REASONS FOR NOT GOING AHEAD WITH IT.

> OWLS OFTEN "T BAR" THEMSELVES! AGAIN, IT IS A GREAT TOOL FOR OWLS, BUT IT WILL BACKFIRE ON YOU WITH ALL THE OTHERS.

YET, WHEN J. DOUGLAS EDWARDS AND OTHERS TO THIS DAY TALK ABOUT MEMORIZING THIS AND USING IT, THEY NEVER (TO MY KNOWLEDGE) MENTION THE WARNING TO ONLY USE IT WITH THE ANALYTICAL OWL PERSONALITY.

> I HAVE WITNESSED SALES LOST BECAUSE OF THIS MISUSE. DON'T FALL INTO THAT CATEGORY.

## "KILLER CLOSES FOR EACH PERSONALITY™" IS THE THIRD DAY SEMINAR IN MY MASTER CLOSER TRILOGY SERIES.

GO AHEAD AND MAKE A LIST OF ALL THE CLOSES YOU KNOW AND USE! WHAT NUMBER DID YOU GET UP TO? GO THROUGH AND MARK WHICH OF THOSE CLOSES WOULD WORK BEST AND WORST FOR EACH ANIMAL PERSONALITY. CAN YOU NAME 46 DIFFERENT CLOSES?

> **USING THE "WRONG CLOSE" FOR A PERSON'S PERSONALITY IS A FIVE ON THE FIVE-TO-ONE "TORTURE SCALE" AND IT JUST DOESN'T MAKE GOOD COMMON SENSE TO DO SO.**

# NOTES

THINGS I AGREE WITH

THINGS I DISAGREE WITH

THINGS I NEED TO WORK ON

ACTION PLAN FOR ME

# CHAPTER 21

## LIE/MYTH #18: CALCULATING CLOSING RATIOS IS NOT REALLY ACCURATE FOR OUR BUSINESS.

I HIGHLY RECOMMEND THAT <u>EVERYONE</u> CALCULATE CLOSING RATIOS 100% OF THE TIME, NO MATTER IF YOU SELL MULTI-MILLION DOLLAR CHEMICAL CONTRACTS, RETAIL OF ANY KIND, NON-TANGIBLE OR TANGIBLE PRODUCTS.

I STILL HAVE SALES MANAGERS THAT TELL ME THEY DON'T BELIEVE IN CLOSING RATIOS BECAUSE THEY ARE NOT ALWAYS ACCURATE. THEY ARE <u>ALWAYS</u> ACCURATE, IF CALCULATED CORRECTLY! OF COURSE, CIRCUMSTANCES ALTER THE CASES, BUT A SALESPERSON AND SALES MANAGER SHOULD KNOW ON A DAILY, WEEKLY, MONTHLY AND YEARLY BASIS, THE TOTAL NUMBER OF PROSPECTS VERSUS THE TOTAL NUMBER OF SALES.

A CLOSING RATIO IS, OF COURSE, THE NUMBER OF BUYING UNITS (TRAFFIC) OR PRESENTATIONS AS IT RELATES TO NET SALES.

DEFINITION OF A BUYING UNIT: IF THERE ARE 3 PEOPLE IN A GROUP THAT YOU ARE GIVING THE PRESENTATION TO, THAT COUNTS AS 1 BUYING UNIT.

"TRAFFIC" INCLUDES ALL TRAFFIC NOT JUST QUALIFIED TRAFFIC.

**THE REASON I AM EMPHASIZING CLOSING RATIOS IS BECAUSE THEY ARE <u>MEASURABLE</u> AND AN INDICATION OF YOUR SUCCESS.**

IF AFTER READING THIS BOOK YOU END UP THINKING DIFFERENTLY ABOUT THE SALES PROCESS, YOU WILL ACTUALLY CHANGE YOUR BEHAVIOR AND THEN DRASTICALLY INCREASE YOUR RESULTS! YOU WILL <u>ALTER</u> YOUR CLOSING RATIO AND BE ON THE ROAD TO BECOMING A MASTER CLOSER.

**THE PURPOSE OF THIS BOOK IS TO GET YOU TO THINK DIFFERENTLY ABOUT THE SALE PROCESS**

# Bulls, Owls, Lambs and Tigers®: Personality Selling™

WE HAVE CLOSING RATIOS FOR MOST ALL INDUSTRIES. LET ME GIVE YOU AN EXAMPLE FROM NEW HOME SALES OUT OF A MODEL COMPLEX.

---

### EXAMPLE:

### OPERATIONAL DEFINITIONS OF

### CLOSING RATIOS

#### FOR THE NEW HOME INDUSTRY

- **MASTER CLOSER** (THE BEST) 1 IN 4 TO 1 IN 5 CLOSING RATIOS
- **EXCELLENT SALESPERSON** 1 IN 10
- **GOOD SALESPERSON** 1 IN 15
- **MEDIOCRE (AVERAGE) SALESPERSON** 1 IN 20
- **CLERK** 1 IN 25
- **BAD CLERK** 1 IN 30+

---

CALCULATE YOUR CLOSING RATIO FOR YOUR INDUSTRY!

WHAT IS THE CLOSING RATIO OF THE BEST IN YOUR COMPANY?

AGAIN:

IF A SALESPERSON IS AT THIS "EXCELLENT" LEVEL 1 IN 10, WHAT DOES THAT MEAN? IT MEANS FOR EVERY 10 PEOPLE THEY SEE (WHETHER QUALIFIED OR NOT) THEY ARE LOSING 9 OUT OF EVERY 10. NOW, OF COURSE, SOME OF THESE "POTENTIAL BUYERS" ARE NOT REALLY POTENTIAL. SOME ARE NOT READY; SOME ARE NOT WILLING AND SOME ARE NOT ABLE (CAN'T EVEN AFFORD A GOOD PEN AND PENCIL SET).

CLOSING RATIOS ARE BASED ON TOTAL TRAFFIC, NOT JUST QUALIFIED TRAFFIC. COUNT ALL BUYING UNITS.

> **MY QUESTION TO YOU IS, IF YOU ARE 1 IN 10 (EXCELLENT) IS THERE SOMETHING/ANYTHING YOU COULD SAY OR DO TO GET JUST 1 OF THOSE 9 THAT GOT AWAY?**

IS THERE ANYTHING FROM THE PREVIOUS 17 LIES/MYTHS THAT YOU COULD APPLY TO GET JUST 1 OF THOSE 9 THAT GOT AWAY?

IF SO, YOU WOULD BE AT A 2 IN 10 OR A 1 IN 5 AND YOU WOULD HAVE LITERALLY DOUBLED YOUR SALES AND WOULD BECOME A MASTER CLOSER (1 IN 5). I MENTION THIS SEVERAL TIMES, BECAUSE IT IS SO IMPORTANT.

GO BACK THROUGH THE PREVIOUS 17 LIES/MYTHS AND CHECK THE ONES THAT YOU THINK COULD SPECIFICALLY MAKE THAT DIFFERENCE IN YOU GETTING ONE OF THOSE 9 THAT GOT AWAY.

IN THE PRECEEDING EXAMPLE:

> **IF A SALESPERSON IS "AVERAGE" (1 IN 20), THEY WILL GET 5 SALES FOR EVERY 100 TRAFFIC UNITS, WHERE A MASTER CLOSER WILL GET 20 SALES OUT OF THE SAME 100 TRAFFIC UNITS.**

> **4 TIMES AS MUCH/EARNING POSSIBLY 4 TIMES AS MUCH**

> *ANOTHER WAY OF LOOKING AT IT IS, THE COMPANY WOULD BE LOSING 75% OF THEIR POTENTIAL SALES, WITH THAT SALESPERSON.*

> **OFTENTIMES A COMPANY HAS A CHOICE OF SPENDING $100,000+ ON MARKETING TO GET MORE TRAFFIC, WHEN REALLY WHAT THEY NEED TO BE CONCENTRATING ON, IS GETTING BETTER CLOSING RATIOS FROM ALL THEIR SALESPEOPLE.**

CALCULATE YOUR CLOSING RATIO!

AGAIN, WHAT IS THE CLOSING RATIO OF THE "BEST OF THE BEST" IN YOUR INDUSTRY AND IN YOUR COMPANY? STRIVE FOR THAT OR BETTER, YOURSELF!

**80/20 RULE**

THERE IS AN OLD LIE/MYTH THAT 20% OF THE SALESPEOPLE IN A COMPANY DO 80% OF THE BUSINESS. I COULD HAVE INCLUDED THAT AS A SEPARATE MYTH.

IT DOES NOT HAVE TO BE THAT WAY AND IN MOST TOP COMPANIES IT IS NOT THAT WAY. WHY WOULD A COMPANY EVEN ALLOW THAT TO HAPPEN? A COMPANY SHOULD KEEP TRAINING AND EVENTUALLY REPLACE NON-PERFORMERS. A COMPANY CAN BE COMPRISED OF ALL MASTER CLOSERS.

# NOTES

THINGS I AGREE WITH

THINGS I DISAGREE WITH

THINGS I NEED TO WORK ON

ACTION PLAN FOR ME

# CHAPTER 22

> # LIE/MYTH #19: IT IS BEST TO ALWAYS HAVE THE PRICE HIGHER THAN WHAT YOU WOULD SELL IT, SO YOU CAN NEGOTIATE THE PRICE LOWER.

THIS IS A VERY CONTROVERSIAL TOPIC WITH COMPANIES, SALES MANAGERS AND SALESPEOPLE IN THIS DAY AND AGE.

THOSE OF YOU WHO HAVE BEEN AROUND A LONG TIME KNOW THAT SOME INDUSTRIES NEVER NEGOTIATED UP UNTIL ABOUT 2007 OR 2008. THEY DIDN'T HAVE TO!

THEN ALONG CAME THE RECESSION AND MANY INDUSTRIES STARTED NEGOTIATING LIKE CRAZY.

> ### I'M SUGGESTING THAT WE COMPLETELY STOP NEGOTIATING.

PLEASE HAVE A MEETING WITH YOUR ENTIRE COMPANY, AND WITH YOUR TOP MANAGEMENT, ABOUT THIS DISCUSSION.

WHEN THE LAST RECESSION STARTED IN APPROXIMATELY 2007 AND 2008 (THE TIMING IS VARIED IN DIFFERENT GEOGRAPHICAL LOCATIONS), MANY COMPANIES HAD TO LITERALLY TAKE A LOSS IN SOME OF THEIR INVENTORY, TO BE ABLE TO SELL. I UNDERSTAND.

THIS IS WHAT I'M SUGGESTING NOW! <u>DO NOT NEGOTIATE AT ALL!</u> DECIDE IN ADVANCE WHAT THE LOWEST PRICE IS THAT YOUR COMPANY WOULD TAKE FOR YOUR PRODUCT, ALLOWING THE PROFIT YOU WANT AS A NET FIGURE, AND THEN STICK WITH THAT NUMBER.

I GET AGGRAVATED WHEN SOME COMPANIES RAISE THE PRICE OF THEIR PRODUCT JUST TO LOWER IT (HOPING AND WISHING FOR THAT HIGHER PRICE).

THIS IS A MYTH, THAT A BUYER <u>HAS TO</u> FEEL GOOD ABOUT NEGOTIATING THE PRICE DOWN AND IF THEY DON'T GET A BETTER PRICE THAN THE "STICKER PRICE," THEY WON'T BUY. NOT TRUE!

LET'S TAKE A LOOK AT HOW EACH OF MY ANIMAL PERSONALITIES REACTS TO NEGOTIATING.

# Bulls, Owls, Lambs and Tigers®: Personality Selling™

> **BULLS AND "CULTURAL BUYERS"**

BULLS, WHO ARE SOME OF THE TOUGHEST NEGOTIATORS, WILL BUY EVEN IF YOU DON'T LOWER THE PRICE.

> TREAT "CULTURAL BUYERS," (WHO ARE, BY THEIR CULTURE, FORCED TO FEEL AS THOUGH THEY HAVE TO NEGOTIATE), AS BULLS.

> **SELLING EXPENSIVE JEWELRY**

> **THE BULLS JUST HAVE TO BE TOLD AND BELIEVE THAT <u>NO ONE ELSE</u> WILL OR CAN GET A BETTER PRICE THAN THEY.**

SALESPERSON SAYS TO THE BULL, AT THE END OF THE GAME OF SELLING, "ON THIS $20,000 PIECE OF JEWELRY YOU ARE ASKING US TO SELL IT TO YOU FOR $15,000." THE ANSWER IS, "NO." "SOME JEWELRY STORES RAISE THEIR PRICE, JUST SO THEY CAN HAVE A 50% PROFIT. THAT'S NOT THE WAY WE DO IT HERE."

"AS I MENTIONED EARLIER, <u>WE DO NOT NEGOTIATE.</u> I HOPE YOU BELIEVE THAT, BECAUSE IT IS TRUE. NO ONE ELSE WILL BE ABLE TO BUY THIS PARTICULAR PIECE OF JEWELRY FOR LESS THAN $20,000." (YOU CAN ONLY SAY THIS IF EVERYONE ON THE MANAGEMENT TEAM, AND OWNERSHIP, AGREES.)

> **IT HAS TO BE COMPETITIVELY PRICED, WITH YOUR DESIRED PROFIT, THEN DON'T NEGOTIATE!**

# Bulls, Owls, Lambs and Tigers®: Personality Selling™

## JEWELRY STORE EXAMPLE

### ON AN EXPENSIVE JEWELRY ITEM

YOU COULD GO ON TO SAY, "YOU ARE WANTING $5,000 LESS THAN THE PRICE FOR WHICH WE WILL SELL IT, AND THE ANSWER AGAIN IS," NO." IF YOU WANTED TO PAY $2,000 OR $1,000 LESS, THE ANSWER WOULD STILL BE "NO!" "AGAIN, IF YOU LIKE THIS BUT DON'T BELIEVE THIS, YOU WILL BUY FROM SOMEONE ELSE AND POSSIBLY BUY SOMETHING THAT YOU DON'T LIKE AS MUCH. I HOPE YOU DON'T, BUT THIS IS THE LOWEST PRICE THAT ANYONE WILL BE ABLE TO BUY IT IN THIS STORE."

> YOU COULD GO ON TO SAY, "WHAT WE HAVE DONE IS NEGOTIATE FOR YOU. SOME JEWELRY STORES RAISE THEIR PRICES ONLY TO LOWER THEM, SO THE BUYER THINKS THEY ARE GETTING A GOOD DEAL. WE HAVE ALREADY NEGOTIATED FOR YOU. THIS IS OUR LOWEST PRICE."

OBVIOUSLY, ALL THAT DIALOGUE WOULD BE TOO LONG FOR A BULL OR MANY OTHERS. OF COURSE, I'M NOT ASKING YOU TO MEMORIZE THAT. THAT WOULD BE AGAINST MY PRINCIPLES. GO THROUGH AND HIGHLIGHT WHAT ASPECTS OF THAT WOULD WORK FOR YOU AND GLEAN THE "CONCEPT."

YOU HAVE TO HAVE THE COOPERATION OF YOUR OWNER AND MANAGER ON THIS, SO YOU ARE ALL "SINGING OUT OF THE SAME HYMNAL."

> YOU CAN DO THAT NO MATTER WHAT YOU SELL.

> **NEVER, NEVER SAY TO ANY POTENTIAL BUYER, "MAKE ME AN OFFER!" OR "WHAT DO YOU HAVE IN MIND?" NEVER!**

I'M THINKING THAT THE EXCEPTION TO THIS IS IN REAL ESTATE RESALES.

I'M SUGGESTING THAT FOR ALL MY ANIMAL PERSONALITIES YOU START OFF BY SAYING "NO," BUT IT'S ALL IN HOW YOU DELIVER THE "NO."

# IT'S ALL IN THE PRESENTATION.

BULLS WANT TO MAKE SURE THAT NO ONE ELSE CAN, OR IS GOING TO, GET A BETTER PRICE. THEY NEGOTIATE "HARD, FAST AND OFTEN."

IF YOU TELL A BULL, "THIS IS THE LOWEST PRICE," AND <u>THEN</u> YOU LOWER IT, IT IS GUARANTEED THEY (THE BULL) WILL NOT BUY FROM YOU TODAY, BECAUSE THEY NOW DON'T BELIEVE YOU.

## OWLS NEGOTIATE WITH LOGIC AND THEY ARE JUST AS TOUGH AS BULLS (OWLS USE LOGIC).

**NEW HOME EXAMPLE**

## OWL SAYS, "THE BUILDER DOWN THE STREET IS OFFERING BASICALLY THIS SAME HOUSE WITH MORE SQUARE FOOTAGE AND IT IS A LOWER PRICE. HOW DO YOU EXPLAIN THAT?"

SALESPERSON REPLIES, "IF IT IS SUCH A BETTER HOME AND AT A BETTER PRICE, WHY DIDN'T YOU BUY IT?"

OWL BUYER SAYS, "I DIDN'T SAY IT WAS A BETTER HOME, JUST LARGER (MORE SQUARE FOOTAGE) AND A LOWER PRICE."

SALESPERSON REPLIES, "LET'S SIT DOWN AND TAKE A LOOK AT BOTH HOMES AND MAKE SURE WE ARE COMPARING APPLES TO APPLES AND ORANGES TO ORANGES. ARE YOU FAMILIAR WITH WHAT IS SOMETIMES CALLED, "THE T-BAR CLOSE OR BEN FRANKLIN CLOSE?"

OWL BUYER SAYS, "OF COURSE."

SALESPERSON, "WELL, LET'S DO THAT IN WRITING WITH BOTH HOMES AND LOOK AT THE VALUE OF EACH."

YOUR THOUGHTS?

# Bulls, Owls, Lambs and Tigers®: Personality Selling™

> **THE TWO BEST NEGOTIATORS ARE BULLS AND OWLS. (NOT NECESSARILY IN THAT ORDER)**
>
> **THE TWO WORST NEGOTIATORS ARE LAMBS AND TIGERS, BUT THEY STILL BOTH "ATTEMPT" TO NEGOTIATE.**

**LAMBS**

LAMB SAYS, "I HAVE BEEN TOLD BY FRIENDS AND RELATIVES NOT TO ACCEPT YOUR ORIGINAL PRICE, SO PLEASE TELL ME IF I CAN GET A BETTER PRICE THAN THIS."

SALESPERSON "NO, I REALLY WOULD LOVE TO DO THAT FOR YOU BUT I REALLY CANNOT LOWER THE PRICE AT ALL. IF I COULD, I WOULD. AS I MENTIONED, THERE IS THIS PUBLICIZED SPECIAL GOING ON UNTIL THE END OF THE THIS MONTH AND THAT IS TRULY THE BEST I CAN DO FOR YOU. ARE YOU READY TO PROCEED?"

> **IT'S THE SAME ANSWER, BUT "IT'S ALL IN THE PRESENTATION!"**

**TIGERS**

> **TIGERS WILL FAKE NEGOTIATION, JUST FOR THE FUN OF THE FAKE! TIGERS FAKE A LOT OF THINGS, JUST FOR THE FUN OF IT.**

© 2021 Charles J. Clarke III. "Bulls, Owls, Lambs and Tigers®" is a registered federal trademark of Charles J. Clarke III since 1988. Personality Selling™ and BOLT™ are Trademarks of Charles J. Clarke III. NO reproduction in any form is allowed.

**Bulls, Owls, Lambs and Tigers®: Personality Selling™**

# RED CORVETTE

TIGER SAYS WHEN BUYING A NEW RED CORVETTE, "I AM NOT GOING TO PAY STICKER PRICE. NO, I'M NOT GOING TO DO IT!"

CAR SALESMAN, "WHY DON'T YOU TAKE IT FOR A DRIVE DOWN THAT ROAD OVER THERE, AND PUNCH IT OUT. FIRST LET'S PUT THE TOP DOWN."

WHEN THE TIGER COMES BACK FROM THE DRIVE, SALESPERSON SAYS "HOW DID IT FEEL? HOW DID THE NEW CAR SMELL? HOW DID IT DRIVE? ARE YOU READY TO GO AHEAD WITH THIS TODAY?"

"SURE." (THE TIGER "FORGOT" ABOUT THE NEGOTIATING.) (THE TRICK NOW IS TO GET THEM FINANCED.)

TIGERS ARE THE WORST NEGOTIATORS BECAUSE THEY GET ALL CAUGHT UP IN THE EMOTIONS OF THE PURCHASES. (OWLS DON'T.)

TOUGH THING ABOUT SELLING TO TIGERS IS GETTING THEM QUALIFIED FOR CREDIT. THAT'S A DISCUSSION FOR A WHOLE OTHER TOPIC. CATCH THEM WHEN THEY HAVE MONEY. IF THEY DON'T NOW, THEY WILL.

PRICING HOMES:

WHILE WE ARE STILL ON PRICING, WHAT'S WITH SOME COMPANIES STILL HAVING HOMES PRICED $199,950 OR $999,950?

FIRST OF ALL, TIGERS THINK IT'S JUST TOO MANY NUMBERS AND BULLS THINK YOU ARE TRYING TO TRICK THEM INTO THINKING THAT IT IS REALLY NOT $200,000 OR A MILLION DOLLARS.

WHEN A COUPLE IS BUYING A MILLION DOLLAR SOMETHING, DO THEY TELL THEIR FRIENDS, "I BOUGHT IT FOR $999,950?" NO! THEY SAY, "WE BOUGHT IT FOR A MILLION."

WE'RE NOT SELLING SHIRTS AT $99 IN ORDER TO **NOT** HAVE IT LOOK LIKE A $100. THE OTHER IS "OLD SCHOOL" THINKING.

# Bulls, Owls, Lambs and Tigers®: Personality Selling™

## THIS NEXT ONE COULD BE A MYTH IN ITSELF.

## "IN NEGOTIATING, WHENEVER YOU ASK A CLOSING QUESTION, SHUT UP. THE FIRST PERSON WHO SPEAKS LOSES!"

**THIS ONE ALONE IS A FIVE ON THE FIVE-TO ONE "TORTURE SCALE," FOR MOST EVERYONE.**

THAT IS JUST NOT TRUE. THAT MYTH CAME FROM J. DOUGLAS EDWARDS IN HIS BOOK, "FOUNDATIONS OF MODERN SELLING." THINK ABOUT THAT! HOW ABSURD!

THAT'S A BULL STATEMENT THAT WHEN USED ON BULLS, IT ONLY MAKES THEM MAD. (IT ALSO ENDS UP IN A "BULL FIGHT." LAMBS, OWLS AND TIGERS HATE IT, AS A BUYER, AND IT MAKES THEM NOT WANT TO BUY.)

IT IS SOMETIMES REFERRED TO AS "F.S.Q.S." (FRIENDLY, SILENT, QUESTIONING, STARE) – THERE'S REALLY NOTHING "FRIENDLY" ABOUT IT!

I RECENTLY WITNESSED THIS. THE BUYER ASKED FOR A LOWER PRICE AND THE SALESPERSON GAVE THEIR LOWER PRICE AND SAID, "WILL THIS WORK FOR YOU?" THE SALESPERSON DIDN'T SAY ANYTHING MORE, NOR DID THE POTENTIAL BUYER. I TIMED IT. THAT "SILENCE" LASTED TWO MINUTES AND THIRTY-FIVE SECONDS. THEN THE POTENTIAL BULL BUYER JUST STOOD UP AND WALKED AWAY.

A FEW DAYS LATER I ASKED THAT SALESPERSON IF THAT POTENTIAL BUYER EVER CAME BACK AND THE SALESPERSON SAID, "NO."

WHY DO WE CONTINUE TO PERPETUATE "LIES AND MYTHS IN SELLING," THAT WERE CREATED OVER 50 YEARS AGO, AND THAT NEVER WORKED? YET WE KEEP ON "PASSING ON" THESE "LIES AND MYTHS" AS IF THEY WERE SACRED. THEY ARE NOT!

THINK HOW A LAMB AND OWL WOULD REACT TO THAT (TOO MUCH PRESSURE OF SILENCE). THEY WOULD REACT BY NOT BUYING.

# Bulls, Owls, Lambs and Tigers®: Personality Selling™

I HAVE HEARD SEVERAL SPEAKERS SAY SOMETHING LIKE THE ONLY PRESSURE THAT SHOULD BE APPLIED IS THE PRESSURE OF SILENCE. I DISAGREE WITH THAT ON TWO LEVELS: 1) WHY SILENCE, AND 2) WHY NOT APPLY PRESSURE IN OTHER WAYS, LIKE URGENCY CLOSES FOR TIGERS AND BULLS? THEY LIKE THAT.

> LET'S GIVE OUR BUYERS MORE "RESPECT" IN THE WAY WE SELL AND NOT TRY TO MANIPULATE THEM. SELL THEM THE WAY THEY WANT TO BE SOLD. THEN MAYBE SOME SALESPEOPLE WILL GIVE YOU MORE "RESPECT," WHEN YOU ARE NEXT BUYING SOMETHING.

PLEASE QUESTION THESE OUTDATED, ARCHAIC SAYINGS AND BELIEFS.

QUESTION EVERYTHING! BECOME THE BEST!

YOU MAY BE SAYING THAT IT HAS WORKED FOR YOU IN THE PAST, BUT HOW MANY DID YOU TORTURE AND LOSE, IN THE PROCESS?

# NOTES

THINGS I AGREE WITH

THINGS I DISAGREE WITH

THINGS I NEED TO WORK ON

ACTION PLAN FOR ME

# CHAPTER 23

> # LIE/MYTH #20: THE MOST IMPORTANT ACCOMPLISHMENT A SALESPERSON CAN ACCOMPLISH, ON THE FIRST VISIT, IS TO GIVE THE BEST PRESENTATION POSSIBLE TO GET THE BUYER EXCITED ENOUGH TO COME BACK.

WE'VE PRETTY MUCH COVERED THAT THE MOST IMPORTANT TASK A SALESPERSON CAN REALLY ACCOMPLISH IS TO <u>CLOSE</u> THEM THAT VERY FIRST DAY. DEPENDING ON YOUR INDUSTRY, 50% OF YOUR SALES COULD BE AND SHOULD BE DONE THE FIRST DAY. HALF OF THE BUYERS (TIGERS AND BULLS) SAY THAT IS THEIR PREFERENCE. SO CLOSE THEM THE WAY <u>THEY</u> WANT TO BE CLOSED.

> **IF THEY LEAVE WITHOUT BUYING, ALWAYS TRY TO HAVE A SCHEDULED "NEXT APPOINTMENT," OR AT LEAST A SCHEDULED "TENTATIVE APPOINTMENT." BUT DON'T BE OBNOXIOUS ABOUT IT.**

IF 50% WON'T BUY THE FIRST DAY, IT MEANS 50% WILL AND WANT TO.

I MENTIONED EARLIER THAT THE AVERAGE "BEEN BACK" RATIO IS ABOUT 8% TO 10%. WITH REALLY GREAT "FOLLOW UP" YOU CAN GET THAT UP TO 16% TO 20%.

> **SOME PORTION OF YOUR BUYERS WILL NOT BUY THE FIRST DAY, SO YOU'D BETTER MAKE SURE YOUR "FOLLOW UP" IS 100% ON THE MONEY.**

I HAVE WORKED WITH SOME SALESPEOPLE WHO HAVE SAID (BEFORE WE REALLY STARTED WORKING TOGETHER) THAT THEIR GOAL WAS TO <u>NOT</u> GET THE APPOINTMENT WHILE THE POTENTIAL BUYER WAS STILL THERE BUT TO CALL THEM THE NEXT DAY AND SET THE APPOINTMENT WHILE ON THE PHONE.

> **SET THE APPOINTMENT WHILE THEY ARE STILL THERE.**

# NOTES

THINGS I AGREE WITH

THINGS I DISAGREE WITH

THINGS I NEED TO WORK ON

ACTION PLAN FOR ME

# CHAPTER 24

# LIE/MYTH #21: 92% OF ALL POTENTIAL BUYERS HAVE BEEN TO YOUR WEBSITE.

I JUST HEARD THIS LIE/MYTH AT A RECENT CONVENTION! WHERE DID THEY COME UP WITH THAT? WHAT SAMPLE DID THEY USE? WHERE WAS IT?

AT THE SAME CONVENTION I HEARD ANOTHER SPEAKER SAY, "83% OF YOUR BUYERS HAVE ALREADY BEEN TO YOUR WEBSITE BEFORE THEY CAME IN."

(SURPRISE! BOTH OF THESE HAPPENED TO HAVE WEBSITE DESIGN BUSINESSES.)

**HERE'S THE TRUTH: WE REALLY DON'T KNOW UNLESS WE ASK.**

SOME INDUSTRIES AND SOME REGIONS REPORT THAT THE NUMBER IS LESS THAN 50% THAT GO TO THEIR WEBSITE.

A LOT OF SALESPEOPLE STILL <u>DON'T</u> ASK THE QUESTION OF EVERYONE, "HAVE YOU BEEN TO OUR WEBSITE? HOW MUCH DO YOU KNOW ABOUT US?" (OF COURSE IN SOME INDUSTRIES THIS WOULD NOT MAKE SENSE.)

EVERYONE SHOULD BE ASKING THOSE TWO QUESTIONS 100% OF THE TIME, IN THE BEGINNING UNDER "QUALIFYING FOR WILLING". IT WILL SAVE YOU A LOT OF TIME NOT TALKING ABOUT WHAT THEY DON'T HAVE AN INTEREST IN.

TIGERS HAVE A HIGH PROBABILITY OF NOT HAVING GONE TO THE WEBSITE FIRST. THEY JUST GO IN. BULLS WILL ALSO DO THIS.

# NOTES

THINGS I AGREE WITH

THINGS I DISAGREE WITH

THINGS I NEED TO WORK ON

ACTION PLAN FOR ME

# CHAPTER 25

## LIE/MYTH #22: ALL BUYERS BUY WITH EMOTION AND JUSTIFY IT WITH LOGIC.

YOU SEE THE TREND HERE. THIS MYTH HAS NEVER MADE SENSE TO ME, BUT IT CERTAINLY DOES GET PERPETUATED.

### TIGERS BUY WITH EMOTION AND JUSTIFY IT WITH EMOTION.

ASK AROUND! SOME PEOPLE WILL JUST NOT BUY WITH EMOTION.

### OWLS BUY WITH LOGIC AND JUSTIFY IT WITH LOGIC.

EVEN IF BUYING AN EMOTIONAL PURCHASE, SUCH AS A HOME, OWLS DO NOT BUY THAT HOME WITH EMOTION. THEY DON'T WANT TO AND THEY DON'T.

**I CRINGE EVERYTIME I HEAR, "ALL BUYERS BUY WITH EMOTION."**

HOW NAIVE!

DO YOU BELIEVE THAT ALL BUYERS BUY WITH EMOTION (NO MATTER WHAT THE PRODUCT IS?)

I KNOW THAT NOT ALL BUYERS BUY WITH EMOTION.

### SELLING FRANCHISES
### EXAMPLE OF A LAND DEAL (100 ACRES) IN PHOENIX

BACK WHEN I WAS WITH TODAY'S AMERICAN BUILDER (STORY EXPLAINED IN CHAPTER 37, MYTH #34), WE WERE TRYING TO GET THIS PARTICULAR BUILDER INVOLVED IN THE FRANCHISE OF TODAY'S AMERICAN BUILDER. THE BUILDER SAID HE FIRST NEEDED TO SECURE THESE 100 ACRES. WE ASKED IF

# Bulls, Owls, Lambs and Tigers®: Personality Selling™

WE COULD DRIVE AROUND THE PERIMETER AND POSSIBLY SOME OF THE INTERIOR OF THE PROPERTY, IN THE JEEP.

HE SAID WE COULD DO THAT, BUT <u>HE</u> DID NOT WANT TO DO THAT, BECAUSE HE HAD ALREADY SEEN THE AERIAL MAPS OF THE TERRAIN, SEEN ALL THE COMPARIBLES AND FINANCIALS, AND HE DID NOT WANT TO <u>TOUR</u> THE PROPERTY.

> **HE SAID, "HE DID NOT WANT TO GET**
>
> **"<u>EMOTIONALLY</u> INVOLVED!"**

IT WAS ONLY ABOUT THE NUMBERS TO HIM AND HE SAID HE <u>ALWAYS</u> GUARDED AGAINST GETTING EMOTIONALLY INVOLVED WHEN BUYING **<u>ANYTHING</u>**, <u>EVEN HIS OWN HOME</u>.

THIS IS NOT AN UNUSUAL CASE. ABOUT 50% OF THE POPULATION (OWLS & BULLS) SAY THEY DO <u>NOT</u> BUY ON EMOTION AND THEY FIND IT VERY AGGRAVATING (TORTURE) WHEN A SALESPERSON TRIES TO GET THEM TO DO SO.

> **THIS IS A SOLID THREE ON THE FIVE-TO-ONE "TORTURE SCALE."**

# NOTES

THINGS I AGREE WITH

THINGS I DISAGREE WITH

THINGS I NEED TO WORK ON

ACTION PLAN FOR ME

## CHAPTER 26

> # LIE/MYTH #23: IN SELLING TO ACTIVE ADULTS (50+ YEARS OF AGE), THEY REALLY NEED TO BE SOLD AND TREATED DIFFERENTLY, AND CERTAINLY WOULDN'T BUY THE FIRST DAY.

WHO MADE UP THAT MYTH?

YES, THE <u>PRODUCT</u> HAS TO BE DIFFERENT, BUT I'M SUGGESTING WHY WOULD YOU SELL TO THEM ANY DIFFERENTLY? AT LEAST 50% DO <u>NOT</u> WANT TO BE SOLD DIFFERENLTY AND ACTUALLY RESENT THAT.

> **YOUNG BULLS, OWLS, LAMBS OR TIGERS® BUYERS GROW UP TO BE OLD BULLS, OWLS, LAMBS AND TIGERS® (BUYERS WITH THE SAME ATTRIBUTES).**

60-YEAR-OLD TIGERS AND BULLS SAY THEY <u>WOULD</u> BUY THE FIRST DAY, AND WOULD PREFER TO DO SO.

| EXAMPLE |
|---|
| DEL WEBB COMMUNITY IN PHOENIX BEFORE IT WAS PART OF PULTE: |

BACK A NUMBER OF YEARS AGO (MAYBE 20 YEARS AGO) MY FRIEND SUE CAMERA, WHO WAS AN EXECUTIVE VICE PRESIDENT WITH THEIR SUN CITY COMMUNITIES, BROUGHT ME IN TO HELP IN CONSULTING AND SEMINARS. UP UNTIL THAT TIME THEY HAD NO SALES DONE THE FIRST DAY.

# Bulls, Owls, Lambs and Tigers®: Personality Selling™

> AFTER APPROXIMATELY 6 MONTHS OF MY COMING IN SEVERAL DAYS EACH MONTH, WE GOT THE NUMBER OF SALES THAT WERE DONE THE "FIRST DAY," TO OVER 35% AND THE TOTAL NUMBER OF <u>SALES MORE THAN DOUBLED EACH MONTH.</u>

**THIS WAS WITH 50+ BUYERS.**

> POINT: IN ACTIVE ADULT COMMUNITIES, IF WE EXPECT THEM <u>NOT</u> TO BUY THE FIRST DAY, THEY WON'T.
>
> WHEN I START TO WORK WITH ACTIVE ADULT COMMUNITIES (50+) IT'S ALWAYS LIKE "DÉJÀ VU" ALL OVER AGAIN, WITH THE SAME MYTH.

**STOP IT!**

AGAIN, THIS WAS APPROXIMATELY 20 YEARS AGO, BUT WE REPEAT THOSE SIMILAR STATISTICS WITH VARIOUS 50+ COMMUNITIES, ALL ACROSS AMERICA, EACH AND EVERY YEAR.

> **NO MATTER WHAT YOU ARE SELLING, SO MANY INDUSTRIES HAVE THIS MYTH, OF "TREAT SENIORS DIFFERENTLY." I ASK, "WHY?"**

YES, GIVE THEM ("US" – I'M INCLUDED HERE), THE <u>"DISCOUNTS,"</u> BUT <u>SELL US</u> THE SAME WAY YOU WOULD SELL EVERYONE ELSE. REMEMBER, "50 IS THE NEW 30," AND "70 IS THE NEW 50." THIS MEANS HOW <u>THEY</u> "PERCEIVE THEMSELVES."

HOW OLD DO YOU PRECEIVE YOURSELF?

HOW MUCH YOUNGER IS THAT, THEN YOU REALLY ARE?

DON'T TORTURE AND <u>INSULT</u> THE 50+ BUYER, BECAUSE OF THIS MYTH.

> **THREE BOMBS ON THE FIVE-TO-ONE "TORTURE SCALE."**

# NOTES

THINGS I AGREE WITH

THINGS I DISAGREE WITH

THINGS I NEED TO WORK ON

ACTION PLAN FOR ME

**Bulls, Owls, Lambs and Tigers®: Personality Selling™**

## CHAPTER 27

# LIE/MYTH #24: SELLING RESORT COMMUNITIES AND GOLF COURSE COMMUNITIES IS VERY DIFFERENT FROM SELLING NON-RESORT COMMUNITIES.

BELIEVE THAT AND YOU WILL SELL LESS.

YOU GET THE POINT!

> THE COMMUNITY AND AMENITIES ARE DIFFERENT BUT THE **"MASTER CLOSER SELLING SKILL SET"** IS THE SAME.

LOTS OF RESORT COMMUNITIES AND GOLF COURSE COMMUNITIES THAT WE WORK WITH ARE SO PROUD OF ALL THEIR AMENITIES, THAT THEY WANT THEIR SALESPEOPLE TO TAKE PROSPECTIVE BUYERS ON A SEVERAL HOUR TOURS SHOWING THEM ALL THE AMENITIES.

FOLLOW MY GUIDELINES FROM MY CHAPTER ON SITTING THEM DOWN FIRST IN CHAPTER 30, MYTH #27.

> BULLS DON'T WANT TO SEE AND HEAR EVERYTHING! THEY JUST CAME IN TO BUY

> OFTEN TIME WE GO "PAST THE CLOSE" AND DESTROY THE SALE.

> ASK THEM HOW THEY WANT TO PROCEED.

> THIS MYTH GOES WAY PAST SELLING GOLF COURSE AND RESORT COMMUNITIES. IT APPLIES TO SELLING ANYTHING!

# Bulls, Owls, Lambs and Tigers®: Personality Selling™

HOW OFTEN HAS YOUR "PROGRAMMED PRESENTATION" GOTTEN IN THE WAY OF ASKING, "WHAT DO YOU THINK ABOUT GOING AHEAD WITH THIS TODAY?" OR "DO YOU WANT TO BUY IT?"

HOW OFTEN HAVE YOU GONE, "PAST THE CLOSE?"

YOUR THOUGHTS?

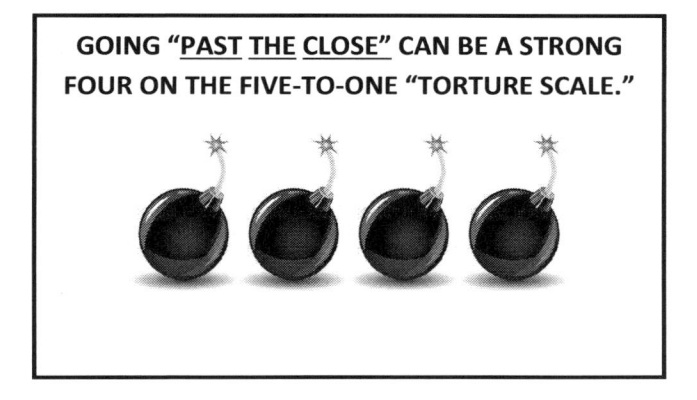

GOING "PAST THE CLOSE" CAN BE A STRONG FOUR ON THE FIVE-TO-ONE "TORTURE SCALE."

# NOTES

THINGS I AGREE WITH

THINGS I DISAGREE WITH

THINGS I NEED TO WORK ON

ACTION PLAN FOR ME

**Bulls, Owls, Lambs and Tigers®: Personality Selling™**

## CHAPTER 28

> # LIE/MYTH #25: THERE ARE LITERALLY OVER 100+ OBJECTIONS TO WHY A POTENTIAL BUYER MIGHT NOT BUY.

IF YOU BELIEVE THIS YOU HAVE JUST COMPLICATED YOUR SELLING LIFE, WAY BEYOND WHAT YOU NEED TO DO.

> # "ALL OBJECTIONS IN SELLING CAN BE BROKEN DOWN TO ONLY 7 OBJECTIONS."
> **CHARLES J. CLARKE III**

> # "THERE ARE ONLY SEVEN OBJECTIONS IN SELLING™ (NO MATTER WHAT YOU ARE SELLING)."
> **CHARLES J. CLARKE III**

PLAY A GAME AND TRY TO LIST "THE ONLY SEVEN OBJECTIONS™." (ACTUALLY, I HAVE NEVER SEEN THIS IN WRITING OR DISCUSSED ANYWHERE, EXCEPT FOR THE WORK I HAVE DONE ON THIS SUBJECT.)

© 2021 Charles J. Clarke III. "Bulls, Owls, Lambs and Tigers®" is a registered federal trademark of Charles J. Clarke III since 1988. Personality Selling™ and BOLT™ are Trademarks of Charles J. Clarke III. NO reproduction in any form is allowed.

# Bulls, Owls, Lambs and Tigers®: Personality Selling™

NOW TAKE A MINUTE AND START LISTING 20+ OBJECTIONS OR SOMETHING THAT BLOCKS SOMEONE FROM BUYING <u>YOUR</u> PRODUCT TODAY.

1.
2.
3.
4.
5.
6.
7.
8.
9.
10.
11.
12.
13.
14.
15.
16.
17.
18.
19.
20.

MORE:

© 2021 Charles J. Clarke III. "Bulls, Owls, Lambs and Tigers®" is a registered federal trademark of Charles J. Clarke III since 1988. Personality Selling™ and BOLT™ are Trademarks of Charles J. Clarke III. NO reproduction in any form is allowed.

**Bulls, Owls, Lambs and Tigers®: Personality Selling™**

HOW MANY DIFFERENT OBJECTIONS DID YOU GET? SOME PEOPLE GET 100+ OBJECTIONS, DEPENDING ON WHAT THEY SELL.

> "ACTUALLY, <u>ALL</u> OBJECTIONS CAN BE BROKEN DOWN TO "THE ONLY SEVEN OBJECTIONS IN SELLING™."
>
> CHARLES J. CLARKE III

### SEVEN OBJECTIONS IN SELLING™

1) NOT READY.

2) NOT WILLING.

3) NOT ABLE.

4) NEED TO TAKE CARE OF SOMETHING FIRST.

   a) GETTING MY MONEY OUT OF A SWISS BANK ACCOUNT.
   b) WAITING FOR MY UNCLE'S INHERITANCE.
   c) IN SELLING HOMES - "I NEED TO SELL MY HOME FIRST."
   d) IN ON-YOUR-LOT SALES IN CUSTOM HOMES - "WE NEED TO FIND A HOMESITE FIRST."

5) YOUR PRICE IS TOO HIGH. THIS IS DIFFERENT FROM #3 WHICH IS "NOT ABLE" (CAN'T AFFORD IT).

6) NEED TO THINK IT OVER.

7) SOMEONE ELSE NEEDS TO APPROVE IT FIRST. (SPOUSE, SOMEONE ELSE, AN ATTORNEY.)

## OBJECTION #1 "NOT READY"

### READY IS ALL ABOUT TIMING

A **READY** BUYER IS SOMEONE WHO SAYS THAT THEY "HAVE" DECIDED TO EVENTUALLY PURCHASE IN THE GENERAL CATEGORY THAT YOU ARE SELLING (NOT NECESSARILY FROM YOU).

A **NOT READY** BUYER IS SOMEONE WHO HAS "NOT DECIDED TO PURCHASE."

IT'S VERY IMPORTANT TO USE A WORKABLE, OPERATIONAL DEFINITION.

## OBJECTION #2 "NOT WILLING"

A **WILLING** BUYER IS ALL ABOUT "PRODUCT;" THEY LIKE WHAT YOU ARE SELLING.

IF THEY DON'T LIKE **YOU**, **YOU** ARE AN EXTENSION OF THE PRODUCT.

A "**NOT WILLING**" BUYER IS "SOMEONE WHO DOESN'T LIKE YOUR PRODUCT." (IT DOESN'T WORK FOR THEM)

**Bulls, Owls, Lambs and Tigers®: Personality Selling™**

---

## OBJECTION #3: "NOT ABLE"

## CAN'T AFFORD IT

## "THEY ARE NOT IN YOUR PRICE RANGE."

---

WOULD YOU ASK SOMEONE (WHO SAID EARLIER THAT THEY COULDN'T AFFORD IT), "WHAT DO YOU THINK ABOUT GOING AHEAD WITH THIS TODAY?"

IF YOU SIGNED THAT COMMITMENT EARLIER, YOU SHOULD, AND WOULD, EVEN IF YOU ARE SELLING A LARGE TICKET ITEM.

YOU NEVER KNOW WHEN THEY MIGHT HAVE A CO-SIGNER OR "MONEY BURIED IN THEIR BACKYARD." BY ASKING THEM IT DOESN'T MEAN YOU HAVE TO WRITE IT UP. YOU ARE JUST FINDING OUT THEIR "INTENTIONS," SO YOU COULD POSSIBLY DO "CREDIT REPAIR" LATER.

YOU CAN ALSO "PAD" YOUR QUESTION BY SAYING SOMETHING LIKE, "I KNOW YOU TOLD ME EARLIER THAT YOU CAN'T AFFORD IT, BUT I JUST NEED TO ASK YOU, 'WHAT DO YOU THINK ABOUT GOING AHEAD WITH THIS TODAY?' (IT'S ALL IN THE PRESENTATION.)"

## OBJECTION #4 "NEED TO TAKE CARE OF SOMETHING ELSE FIRST"

## OBJECTION #5 "YOUR PRICE IS TOO HIGH"

THIS IS NOT ABOUT BEING "ABLE." IT IS ABOUT THEIR *PERCEPTION* OR POSSIBLY THEM TRYING TO NEGOTIATE.

## OBJECTION #6 "WE NEED TO THINK IT OVER"

(THIS IS A REAL OBJECTION, NOT A SMOKE SCREEN.) WRITE IT UP "SUBJECT TO THINKING IT OVER WITHIN 24 HOURS."

---

© 2021 Charles J. Clarke III. "Bulls, Owls, Lambs and Tigers®" is a registered federal trademark of Charles J. Clarke III since 1988. Personality Selling™ and BOLT™ are Trademarks of Charles J. Clarke III. NO reproduction in any form is allowed.

# Bulls, Owls, Lambs and Tigers®: Personality Selling™

## OBJECTION #7 "MY SPOUSE (OR SOMEONE ELSE) NEEDS TO SEE IT OR APPROVE IT."

WRITE IT UP "SUBJECT TO SPOUSE SEEING IT WITHIN 24 HOURS."

**ASSIGNMENT:** ONCE A PERSON HAS LEFT AND THEY DIDN'T BUY FROM YOU, WRITE DOWN WHICH <u>OBJECTION</u> IT WAS. (WHY THEY DIDN'T BUY.)

***CHALLENGE TO YOU***: *TRY TO COME UP WITH AN OBJECTION THAT DOES <u>NOT</u> FIT INTO ONE OF THESE CATEGORIES. YOU WON'T BE ABLE TO DO THAT.*

# NOTES

THINGS I AGREE WITH

THINGS I DISAGREE WITH

THINGS I NEED TO WORK ON

ACTION PLAN FOR ME

# Bulls, Owls, Lambs and Tigers®: Personality Selling™

## CHAPTER 29

## LIE/MYTH #26: SELLING "HIGH END" PRODUCT IS DIFFERENT FROM SELLING "LOWER END" PRODUCT

### ANSWER: REALLY?

YOU'VE GOT THE POINT BY NOW.

IN MY SEMINARS AND CONSULTING, THIS QUESTION ALWAYS COMES UP IN SOME FORM OR ANOTHER. "ISN'T IT MORE DIFFICULT TO SELL HIGH-END PRODUCT?" OR THE REVERSE OF THAT IS, "ISN'T IT MORE DIFFICULT TO SELL LOW-END PRODUCT?" MY ANSWER IS IT IS THE SAME SKILL SET, AND MY **BOLT™** PERSONALITIES COME INTO PLAY IN THE SAME WAY.

THE "BLOCK" IS OFTEN IN THE MIND OF THE SALESPERSON WHEN THEY SHIFT FROM ONE PRODUCT OR PRICE POINT TO THE NEXT. THE SAME PERCENTAGE OF BUYERS BUYING THE FIRST DAY (APPROXIMATELY 33% TO 50%) REMAIN THE SAME. THE OBJECTION IS NOT WITH THE PRODUCT, BUT WITH THE SALESPERSON.

THIS NEXT STATEMENT COULD ACTUALLY BE A MYTH OF ITS OWN: "OUR CITY OR OUR STATE, OR OUR AREA IS DIFFERENT FROM ANYWHERE ELSE." MY ANSWER TO THAT IS "**NOT REALLY!**"

ALMOST EVERYWHERE I GO, I GET THIS STATEMENT: "CHARLES, YOUR PRINCIPLES ARE SOLID EVERYWHERE ELSE, BUT IT'S DIFFERENT HERE." AGAIN, IF YOU REALLY BELIEVE THAT IT WILL ONLY INTERFERE WITH YOUR SELLING.

NO MATTER WHERE YOU ARE SELLING: LOS ANGELES, CALIFORNIA; BATON ROUGE, LOUISIANA; NEW YORK; CEDAR RAPIDS, IOWA; COLUMBUS, OHIO OR KINGSPORT, TENNESSEE, THE SELLING PRINCIPLES ARE THE SAME.

> **THE SELLING PROCESS IS NOT GENDER BIASED, CITY BIASED, PRODUCT BIASED OR PRICE BIASED. SELLING IS SELLING! THE PRODUCT IS DIFFERENT BUT THE SELLING PROCESS REMAINS THE SAME.**

# Bulls, Owls, Lambs and Tigers®: Personality Selling™

I WAS CONSULTING WITH A JEWELRY STORE, AND BEFORE I STARTED WORKING WITH THEM, THEY HAD THE SELLING PRINCIPLES REVERSED. IT WAS ONE OF THEIR MYTHS THAT HIGHER-PRICED JEWELRY WOULD TAKE AT LEAST TWO VISITS OR MORE TO SELL. THEY HAD A WIDE VARIETY OF EXPENSIVE WATCHES WHICH INCLUDED PRESIDENTIAL ROLEX WATCHES.

THE SALESPEOPLE SAID THEY HAD NEVER SOLD ANY OF THESE WATCHES THE FIRST DAY, BECAUSE ON HIGHER-END JEWELRY, PEOPLE NEEDED TO COME BACK AT LEAST A SECOND TIME IF NOT MORE.

WHOSE OBJECTION WAS THAT?

IT WAS THEIR OBJECTION (SALESPERSON AND THE COMPANY), ACTUALLY, ON HIGHER TICKET ITEMS. BULLS AND TIGERS ARE MORE ATTRACTED TO THEM, BECAUSE THAT PRODUCT IS STRIKING, IMPRESSIVE AND MAKES A STATEMENT (BULLS) AND IS FUN, EXCITING AND DIFFERENT (TIGERS).

AGAIN, BOTH TIGERS AND BULLS (BOTH BEING HIGH RISK TAKERS), HAVE A HIGHER PROBABILITY OF BUYING THE FIRST DAY AND NOT COMING BACK THE SECOND TIME.

DO YOU BELIEVE THAT?

IT'S TRUE!

**YACHTS AND OTHER LUXURY PURCHASES**

> THE SAME PROCESS APPLIES TO BUYING YACHTS AND OTHER LUXURY ITEMS. THERE ARE SOME VERY SUCCESSFUL YACHT SALESPEOPLE WHO REPORT A 80% FIRST DAY BUY. THEY ARE MASTER CLOSERS. THEY MIGHT BE MISSING OWLS AND LAMBS.

YOUR THOUGHTS?

IF YOU GET THIS MYTH CONFUSED, IT WILL BE A TORTURE FOR YOU AND YOUR COMPANY, IN LOST SALES.

# NOTES

THINGS I AGREE WITH

THINGS I DISAGREE WITH

THINGS I NEED TO WORK ON

ACTION PLAN FOR ME

# Bulls, Owls, Lambs and Tigers®: Personality Selling™

## CHAPTER 30

> # LIE/MYTH #27: IT IS BETTER TO ASK QUALIFYING QUESTIONS STANDING UP, RATHER THAN ASKING THEM TO COME INTO YOUR OFFICE AND SIT DOWN (FOR THE FIRST COUPLE MINUTES).

OF COURSE, ON THIS ONE, IT DEPENDS ON WHAT YOU ARE SELLING. IF YOU ARE SELLING CLOTHING IN A RETAIL STORE, YOU WOULDN'T WANT TO DO THIS. HOWEVER, IF YOU ARE SELLING: INDUSTRIAL EQUIPMENT, YACHTS, NEW HOMES, EXISTING HOMES, EXPENSIVE JEWELRY, LARGE CHEMICAL CONTRACTS, ETC. SIT DOWN AND QUALIFY FOR READY, WILLING AND ABLE.

THIS MYTH IS QUITE HUGE, BECAUSE I REALLY BELIEVE MOST INDUSTRIES HAVE BEEN DOING THIS "THING" OF QUALIFYING (SO IMPORTANT) VERY WRONG FOR DECADES. IT HAS JUST KEPT PERPETUATING FROM ONE DECADE TO THE NEXT.

WE ALL KNOW THERE IS THE CRITICAL PATH OF SELLING AND AS DISCUSSED, IT HAS BEEN IN EXISTENCE FOR WELL OVER 100 YEARS. MOST INDUSTRIES REALLY DO NOT FOLLOW IT, THE WAY IT WAS LAID OUT.

> **SCENARIO #1 – (BAD VERSION) –NOT HOW TO DO IT**

SALESPERSON WELCOMES THE PROSPECTIVE BUYER TO THEIR SHOWROOM AND SAYS SOMETHING LIKE, "IS THIS YOUR FIRST TIME IN?"

PROSPECTIVE BUYER SAYS, "YES."

THEN THE SALESPERSON POSITIONS HIMSELF OR HERSELF AROUND THE SELLING TABLE AND STARTS TALKING.

"SINCE THIS IS YOUR FIRST TIME HERE, LET ME TELL YOU A LITTLE ABOUT OUR COMPANY AND THE WAY WE DO THINGS HERE. THEN WE CAN WALK AROUND AND I'LL POINT OUT SOME SPECIFICS."

HOW MANY OF YOU KNOW THAT THAT PARTICULAR PRESENTATION IS GOING ON IN YOUR CITY TODAY? NOT WITH YOU, OF COURSE, BUT WITH OTHERS.

MAYBE YOU DON'T DO IT THAT WAY, BUT THAT IS WHAT IS BEING DONE AND EVEN BEING TAUGHT TO DO, IN MANY COMPANIES.

© 2021 Charles J. Clarke III. "Bulls, Owls, Lambs and Tigers®" is a registered federal trademark of Charles J. Clarke III since 1988. Personality Selling™ and BOLT™ are Trademarks of Charles J. Clarke III. NO reproduction in any form is allowed.

# Bulls, Owls, Lambs and Tigers®: Personality Selling™

LET'S LOOK AT THAT FROM STRICTLY A CRITICAL PATH PRESENTATION.

### CRITICAL PATH AGAIN

1) MEET, GREET AND CONNECT WITH THEM

2) QUALIFY FOR
   A) READY
   B) WILLING
   C) ABLE

3) DEMONSTRATE

4) SELECTION

5) OVERCOME OBJECTIONS AND CLOSE THE SALE

ANALYZE WHAT TOOK PLACE IN THE SITUATION I JUST LAID OUT.

THEY DID A MEETING AND GREETING, NO CONNECTION, AND THEN WENT RIGHT INTO DEMONSTRATING WITHOUT ANY QUALIFYING.

### SCENARIO #2 – (BAD VERSION) – **REALLY** NOT HOW TO DO IT

"WELCOME. IS THIS YOUR FIRST TIME HERE? (IF YES) THEN WHY DON'T YOU LOOK AROUND AND THEN I'LL ANSWER ANY OF YOUR QUESTIONS."

AND IT GOES ON FROM THERE.

LOOK AT WHAT IS MISSING. NO CONNECTION AND NO QUALIFYING FOR READY. JUST JUMPING RIGHT INTO THE PRODUCT, WITHOUT EVEN KNOWING REALLY WHY THEY ARE THERE OR IF THEY ARE REALLY THINKING ABOUT BUYING OR HAVE THEY DECIDED TO BUY?

RE-THINK ABOUT DOING IT THE FOLLOWING WAY. (IT WORKS!)

*FROM CHARLES J. CLARKE III, "THE ART OF ASKING QUESTIONS™"*

**Bulls, Owls, Lambs and Tigers®: Personality Selling™**

## BOX #1: QUALIFYING FOR READY

DEPENDING ON WHAT YOU ARE SELLING, IF THEY ARE COMING TO YOU:

*"WELCOME! HELLO! I AM, (YOUR NAME), AND YOU ARE?"*

*WHEN THEY FIRST COME IN:*

1) "WHAT BRINGS YOU OUT LOOKING AT OUR _____ , TODAY?"

2) "COME ON INTO MY OFFICE AND LET ME FIND OUT MORE ABOUT YOUR NEEDS."

WAIT FOR AN ANSWER.

*IN THE OFFICE (OR SITTING DOWN SOMEWHERE) CONNECT WITH THEM. START TAKING NOTES ON THE REGISTRATION OR INFORMATION CARD, THAT YOU FILL OUT:*

3) "HOW LONG HAVE YOU BEEN LOOKING FOR_____?"

4) "WHAT IS YOUR SITUATION, ARE YOU NEW TO THE AREA?"

5) "WHERE DO YOU CURRENTLY LIVE?"

*6) "ARE YOU "THINKING" ABOUT BUYING OR HAVE YOU ALREADY DECIDED TO PURCHASE?"

*7) "WHEN WOULD YOU LIKE TO ACTUALLY OWN THIS (OR HAVE WORK DONE, OR WHATEVER IS APPROPRIATE FOR YOUR SITUATION?)"

**YOU CAN GET 90% TO COME INTO YOUR OFFICE (OR SIT DOWN). IT WORKS BETTER THAN QUALIFYING STANDING UP. IT WORKS BETTER THAN JUST "TALKING" ABOUT YOUR PRODUCT.**

## Bulls, Owls, Lambs and Tigers®: Personality Selling™

I'M NOT SUGGESTING YOU DO THESE QUESTIONS VERBATIM, BUT JUST HAVE THE GENERAL FLOW. IF YOU ARE IN THEIR OFFICE, YOU STILL START WITH QUALIFYING FOR READY, WILLING AND ABLE INSTEAD OF STARTING WITH TALKING ABOUT YOUR PRODUCT.

BULLS <u>WILL</u> COME INTO YOUR OFFICE (OR SIT DOWN), IF YOU SAY SOMETHING LIKE, "COME ON INTO MY OFICE AND LET ME QUICKLY FIND OUT MORE ABOUT YOUR NEEDS, SO I DON'T TALK ABOUT A LOT OF 'STUFF' IN WHICH YOU HAVE NO INTEREST, AND THEN I'LL SHOW YOU OUR PRODUCT."

**REMEMBER BULLS DON'T GO OUT TO SHOP; THEY GO OUT TO BUY.**

## BOX #2: QUALIFYING FOR WILLING

*DURING THIS TIME, IF YOU USE A REGISTRATION CARD, START FILLING OUT THE CARD YOURSELF. (NOT ASKING THEM TO FILL IT OUT – YOU GET MORE ACCURACY THIS WAY.)*

1. "WHAT ARE YOUR NEEDS, OR ANYTHING ELSE THAT CAN HELP ME, HELP YOU?"
2. "HAVE YOU BEEN TO OUR WEBSITE?"
3. "WHICH ASPECT OR PRODUCT DID YOU LIKE BEST?"

## BOX #3: QUALIFYING FOR ABLE

1. "OUR PRICE RANGE FOR THAT IS $_____ TO OVER $_____.
2. "WHAT PRICE RANGE DID YOU HAVE IN MIND?"
3. **(ON LARGER TICKET ITEMS LIKE CARS, HOMES, OR INDUSTRIAL EQUIPMENT, ETC.)** "WOULD YOU BE PAYING CASH OR WOULD YOU WANT TO HAVE IT FINANCED?"
4. "HAVE YOU BEEN PRE-QUALIFIED?"

© 2021 Charles J. Clarke III. "Bulls, Owls, Lambs and Tigers®" is a registered federal trademark of Charles J. Clarke III since 1988. Personality Selling™ and BOLT™ are Trademarks of Charles J. Clarke III. NO reproduction in any form is allowed.

**Bulls, Owls, Lambs and Tigers®: Personality Selling™**

## BOX #4: HOW WOULD YOU LIKE TO PROCEED?

THESE FIRST "4 BOXES" ARE THE <u>"BEGINNING"</u> OF THE GAME OF SELLING.

### ON "BIG TICKET" ITEMS

WHAT PERCENTAGE OF ALL YOUR POTENTIAL BUYERS DO YOU THINK WILL COME IN TO YOUR OFFICE OR SIT DOWN? I USUALLY GET GUESSES OF ABOUT 50%. YOU WILL GET 90%+ OF ALL YOUR POTENTIAL BUYERS TO COME INTO YOUR OFFICE OR SIT DOWN FOR <u>REAL</u> QUALIFYING, NOT JUST QUALIFYING WHILE THEY ARE BEING DISTRACTED BY YOU, TRYING TO DEMONSTRATE AT THE SAME TIME.

ALL OWLS AND LAMBS WILL COME IN.

---

WILL BULLS COME IN? CERTAINLY.

AGAIN: "COME ON INTO MY OFFICE. LET ME FIND OUT A LITTLE MORE ABOUT YOUR NEEDS, SO I DON'T WASTE YOUR TIME TALKING ABOUT A BUNCH OF STUFF IN WHICH YOU HAVE NO INTEREST."

---

BULLS DO NOT GO OUT TO "SHOP," THEY GO OUT TO "BUY."

IN THIS SYSTEM, FOR THE FIRST 3 MINUTES (APPROXIMATELY) YOU ARE NOT SELLING AT ALL. YOU ARE NOT <u>TELLING</u> ABOUT YOUR PRODUCT, UNLESS THEY ASK. YOU ARE DEVOTING ALL YOUR ATTENTION TO FINDING OUT THEIR <u>READY</u>, <u>WILLING</u> & <u>ABLE</u> NEEDS.

---

### #5: DEMONSTRATION – THE <u>"MIDDLE"</u> OF THE GAME OF SELLING

## TELLING AND SHOWING ALL ABOUT YOUR PRODUCT AND ANSWERING THEIR QUESTIONS

---

BOXES 6 THOUGH 8 ON "OVERCOMING OBJECTIONS/<u>CLOSING THE SALE</u>" AND THE "2ND CHANCE CLOSE" ARE ALL PART OF THE <u>"END"</u> OF THE GAME OF SELLING.

---

© 2021 Charles J. Clarke III. "Bulls, Owls, Lambs and Tigers®" is a registered federal trademark of Charles J. Clarke III since 1988. Personality Selling™ and BOLT™ are Trademarks of Charles J. Clarke III. NO reproduction in any form is allowed.

## 3 PARTS OF THE GAME OF SELLING™

1. <u>BEGINNING</u>
   - QUALIFY FOR READY, WILLING, & ABLE
   - ASK THEM HOW <u>THEY</u> WANT TO PROCEED

2. <u>MIDDLE</u>
   - TELL ABOUT YOUR COMPANY
   - DEMONSTRATE YOUR PRODUCT

3. <u>END</u>
   - SELECT
   - OVERCOME OBJECTIONS
   - CLOSE THE SALE

# PRACTICE, DRILL AND REHEARSE METHODICALLY UNTIL IT BECOMES NATURAL FOR YOU.

# NOTES

THINGS I AGREE WITH

THINGS I DISAGREE WITH

THINGS I NEED TO WORK ON

ACTION PLAN FOR ME

# Bulls, Owls, Lambs and Tigers®: Personality Selling™

## CHAPTER 31

> **LIE/MYTH #28: IF THE BUYER IS READY, WILLING AND ABLE AND SAYS, "NO, THEY DO NOT WANT TO GO AHEAD WITH THIS TODAY," IT WOULD BE RUDE AND PUSHY TO BRING OUT THE PURCHASE AGREEMENT (CONTRACT) AND START WRITING.**

**EXAMPLE OF: SELLING NEW HOMES**

SEE WHAT YOU THINK OF THE <u>FLOW</u> OF THIS.

REMEMBER, THIS IS WITH A

**3 GREEN DOT BUYER**

**3 GREEN DOTS: READY, WILLING AND ABLE BUYER**

THEY SAID THEY HAD 1) DECIDED TO MOVE, 2) THEY LIKED YOUR COMMUNITY, HOME, AND HOME SITE, AND 3) THEY CAN AFFORD IT, BUT WHEN YOU SAID, "WHAT DO YOU THINK ABOUT GOING AHEAD WITH THIS TODAY?" THEY SAY "NO," <u>AFTER</u> YOU ASK THEM THE "5 MAGIC QUESTIONS™."

**BOX #6: FIVE MAGIC QUESTIONS™:**

> *At the home they have chosen, a home under construction, or the home site:*
>
> **You Ask: The Five Magic Questions™:**
>
> - How do you like this community?
> - Is it a community you would like to live in?
> - Which of our homes do you like best for your needs?
> - Is this a home you would like to own?
> - **"What Do You Think About Going Ahead With This Today™?"**

---

© 2021 Charles J. Clarke III. "Bulls, Owls, Lambs and Tigers®" is a registered federal trademark of Charles J. Clarke III since 1988. Personality Selling™ and BOLT™ are Trademarks of Charles J. Clarke III. NO reproduction in any form is allowed.

# Bulls, Owls, Lambs and Tigers®: Personality Selling™

### BOX #7: COME BACK TO MY OFFICE

If the answer is yes, go back to your office and write it up. **IF THE ANSWER IS NO,**

- **YOU ASK "WHY" TO FLUSH OUT THE OBJECTION.**
- **\*COME ON BACK TO MY OFFICE AND LET ME GIVE YOU SOME ADDITIONAL INFORMATION FOR YOU TO TAKE HOME WITH YOU!**
- **\*AND AT THAT TIME, I WILL SHOW YOU OUR "PURCHASE AGREEMENT" FOR IF AND WHEN YOU EVER PURCHASE HERE, YOU WILL KNOW WHAT IT LOOKS LIKE.**

### BOX #8: CONTRACT "Second Chance Close™"

*Back at the office where they have already been:*

**\*AS I HAVE MENTIONED: THIS IS OUR PURCHASE AGREEMENT THAT I SAID I WAS GOING TO SHOW YOU! Let me just fill in 3 lines so you can take it home and know what it looks like.**

1. This is the address of that property. (Start with the address.)
2. This is the price of the home that you liked.
3. This is the earnest money (deposit).

At the bottom of the purchase agreement, I wrote "Subject to: (Their Objection)"

- Subject to spouse approval within 24 hours.
- Subject to thinking it over within 24 hours.
- Subject to whatever their objection was.

You're not being pushy; you are just giving them a SECOND chance to say "Yes" with a "Subject To."

*You can have any combination of these. You always have to have an ending date! If they don't want to sign it, you still give them a copy of it and you have increased the probability they will come back. Before they leave, you put their names at the top.*

AGAIN, EVEN IF THEY DO NOT SIGN, YOU HAVE INCREASED THE "PROBABILITY" THAT THEY WILL COME BACK BECAUSE YOU HAVE PERSONALIZED THE PURCHASE AGREEMENT WITH THEIR NAME AND THEIR ADDRESS OF THE PROPERTY THEY CHOSE. OF COURSE, THERE ARE MORE DETAILS TO BE EXPLAINED ABOUT THIS, BUT THE POINT IS START WRITING IT UP WITH 3 GREEN DOT BUYERS.

© 2021 Charles J. Clarke III. "Bulls, Owls, Lambs and Tigers®" is a registered federal trademark of Charles J. Clarke III since 1988. Personality Selling™ and BOLT™ are Trademarks of Charles J. Clarke III. NO reproduction in any form is allowed.

# Bulls, Owls, Lambs and Tigers®: Personality Selling™

USE THE PURCHASE AGREEMENT AS A TOOL.

"STRETCH THE RUBBER BAND, BUT DON'T BREAK IT."

THIS "SECOND CHANCE CLOSE" IS OBVIOUSLY **NOT FOOL PROOF,** BUT DO YOU THINK IT WOULD INCREASE THE PROBABILITY OF THEM ACTUALLY SIGNING?

AFTER THEY HAVE SAID "NO," WHILE BACK AT THE PROPERTY, MANY SALESPEOPLE MAKE THE MISTAKE OF SAYING: "THIS IS WHAT WE COULD DO. WE COULD WRITE THIS UP, SUBJECT TO YOUR SPOUSE'S APPROVAL."

THE DIFFERENCE BETWEEN THAT AND WHAT I AM SUGGESTING IS,

**WHILE YOU ARE BACK AT THE OFFICE, LOOKING AT THE PURCHASE AGREEMENT WITH YOUR BUYER, YOU SAY:**

"THIS IS WHAT I HAVE DONE."

WHICH HAS THE HIGHER PROBABILITY OF GOING THROUGH?

AN EXAMPLE WOULD BE YOU ARE AT A RESTAURANT AND THE WAITER ASKS IF YOU CARE FOR A DESSERT.

I COULD BRING OUT THE DESSERT TRAY VERSUS

"THIS IS WHAT I HAVE DONE"

"HERE IS THE DESSERT TRAY"

THEN GOING AHEAD AND EXPLAINING THE DESSERT TRAY.

WHICH IS MORE POWERFUL?

**WE DO NOT USE THE "PURCHASE AGREEMENT" OR "ORDER FORM," ENOUGH, AS A CLOSING TOOL. START WRITING! CHARLES J. CLARKE III**

WHEN SOME SALESPEOPLE FIRST HEAR THIS SECOND CHANCE CLOSE, THEY THINK IT IS <u>TOO PUSHY</u>.

YOUR THOUGHTS?

IT'S ALL IN THE PRESENTATION!

# Bulls, Owls, Lambs and Tigers®: Personality Selling™

## REVIEW OF MY 8 BOXES

---

**THE BEGINNING OF THE GAME OF SELLING**

ARE DONE <u>IN YOUR OFFICE</u> (3 TO 5 MINUTES) – (WITH BULLS 2 MINUTES)

---

**BOX #1**: QUALIFY FOR <u>READY</u> (WHILE SITTING DOWN)

**BOX #2:** QUALIFY FOR <u>WILLING</u> (WHILE SITTING DOWN)

(START FILLING OUT REGISTRATION CARD)

**BOX #3:** QUALIFY FOR <u>ABLE</u> (WHILE SITTING DOWN)

**BOX #4**: "HOW WOULD YOU LIKE TO PROCEED?" GIVE THEM CHOICES

---

**THE MIDDLE OF THE GAME OF SELLING**

**BOX #5:** DEMONSTRATION (ALL ABOUT YOUR COMPANY AND YOUR PRODUCT)

PROCEEDING THE WAY <u>THEY</u> WANT TO PROCEED

---

**THE END OF THE GAME OF SELLING**

**BOX #6:** THE FIVE MAGIC QUESTIONS WITH <u>ALL,</u> EVEN "3 RED DOT" BUYERS (NOT READY, NOT WILLING, NOT ABLE)

**BOX #7:** BACK TO YOUR OFFICE EITHER TO WRITE IT UP OR TO GO OVER THE CONTRACT.

**BOX #8:** "SECOND CHANCE CLOSE™ "(THIS ACTUALLY IS WHEN CLOSING REALLY BEGINS.)

---

**BOX 8 IS WHERE YOU WOULD REALLY USE YOUR SKILL SET WITH "KILLER CLOSES FOR DIFFERENT PERSONALITIES™.**

# Bulls, Owls, Lambs and Tigers®: Personality Selling™

REMEMBER A 3 GREEN DOT BUYER IS READY, WILLING AND ABLE, (<u>EVEN</u> IF THEY HAVE AN OBJECTION: WE NEED TO SELL OUR HOME, SPOUSE IS NOT HERE, MY ATTORNEY NEEDS TO SEE THE CONTRACT FIRST, WE DON'T HAVE OUR LAND (OR YOUR LOT BUYERS OF A CUSTOM HOME), WE NEED TO THINK IT OVER, WE HAVEN'T DECIDED WHICH OF YOUR HOMES IS BEST FOR US, WE DON'T KNOW WHAT AMENITIES TO CHOOSE, WE HAVE MORE QUESTIONS, ETC.)

> **ASKING A POTENTIAL BUYER, "<u>WHAT DO YOU THINK ABOUT GOING AHEAD WITH THIS TODAY™</u>?" IS ONLY THE "<u>BEGINNING</u>".  IT'S ONLY A "TRIAL CLOSE" LIKE "HOW DO YOU LIKE THESE CABINETS?"  IF YOU THINK OF IT LIKE THAT, YOU CAN DO IT WITH EVERYONE, EVEN THREE RED DOTS. (N0T READY, NOT WILLING, NOT ABLE.)**

> **"REAL CLOSING" IS UNDER BOX #8 WITH 3 GREEN DOT BUYERS WHO ARE STILL SAYING "NO."  THIS IS THE BIG CHALLENGE OF A MASTER CLOSER.**

YOUR THOUGHTS?

### SELLING LANDSCAPE

WE WERE BUYING A LARGE LANDSCAPE PACKAGE AT APPROXIMATELY $150,000 FOR A COMMUNITY FOR WHICH I WAS CONSULTING.  WE HAD NO INTENTIONS OF PURCHASING IT THAT FIRST DAY WE LOOKED.

THE SALESPERSON ASKED IF WE WANTED TO GO AHEAD WITH THE PURCHASE AND THE THREE OF US WHO WERE INVOLVED, SAID, "NO."

WE WENT OUT TO THE NURSERY AND LOOKED AT ALL THE LANDSCAPING CHOICES AND HE KEPT WRITING DOWN WHAT WE LIKED.  HE ASKED IF WE WANTED TO BUY TODAY AND WE SAID, "NO, NOT TODAY." HE SAID, "LET'S GO BACK INTO MY OFFICE AND LET ME GIVE YOU A 'SUMMARY' OF MY NOTES ON WHAT YOU HAVE CHOSEN, OR LIKED, TODAY."

## Bulls, Owls, Lambs and Tigers®: Personality Selling™

WHEN WE GOT BACK TO HIS OFFICE (BY THE CASH REGISTER) HE STARTED WRITING THE SUMMARY ON "THE ORDER FORM" WHICH TURNED OUT TO BE SEVERAL PAGES.

HE WROTE THE ITEMS ALONG WITH THE PRICES, TOTALED EVERYTHING UP, PUT THE 10% DISCOUNT THAT HE TALKED ABOUT FROM THE BEGINNING, AND PUT DOWN THE DELIVERY DATE.

**ALL THIS WAS <u>AFTER</u> WE HAD SAID, "NO."**

HE THEN SAID, "I DID HEAR YOU SAY NO" (HE "PADDED" THE OBJECTION), "BUT HERE IT IS IN WRITING AND IF YOU WRITE A $10,000 CHECK TODAY, WE CAN HAVE IT DELIVERED BY THE ABOVE DATE. OK?"

THE THREE OF US LOOKED AT EACH OTHER, AND SAID, "WHY NOT?"

WE DID IT!

IF HE HAD NOT "WRITTEN IT UP," WE WOULD NOT HAVE DONE IT THAT DAY AND MAYBE WE WOULD NOT HAVE BOUGHT FROM HIM AT ALL. SOME BUYERS WOULD NOT BE COMFORABLE WITH DOING THIS. WE WERE, BECAUSE HE AT LEAST GAVE US AN "OPPORTUNITY" TO SAY YES. IF UNDER THE SAME CIRCUMSTANCES, LET'S SAY WE SAID "NO" (WE DIDN'T) HE COULD HAVE EVENTUALLY GIVEN US A COPY OF WHAT HE HAD WRITTEN. WOULD THAT HAVE INCREASED THE PROBABLITY OF US COMING BACK?

> **WRITING SOMETHING UP, EVEN AFTER THEY HAVE SAID, "NO," IS A POWERFUL TOOL!**

HOW CAN <u>YOU</u> USE THIS TOOL?

THIS IS REALLY <u>NOT</u> PUSHY, IT IS "THOROUGH." IT'S ALL IN THE PRESENTATION.

# NOTES

THINGS I AGREE WITH

THINGS I DISAGREE WITH

THINGS I NEED TO WORK ON

ACTION PLAN FOR ME

# CHAPTER 32

> # LIE/MYTH #29: WHEN SELLING AUTOMOBILES, VANS, OR TRUCKS, A SALESPERSON SHOULD ALWAYS GET THE POTENTIAL BUYER TO DRIVE IT FIRST.

DEPENDING ON IF YOU ARE ACTUALLY IN AUTOMOBILE SALES OR NOT, YOUR ANSWER MIGHT BE DIFFERENT.

> **EXAMPLE #1**
>
> "LET ME GET THE KEYS, YOU HAVE TO DRIVE IT FIRST."

A NUMBER OF YEARS AGO WE WERE LIVING IN TAMPA BAY, FLORIDA, AND I SAW A TELEVISION AD THAT SAID, "COME OUT THIS WEEKEND AND BUY A VAN. PAY ONLY 2% FINANCING."

NOW, OF COURSE, TODAY IT IS SOMETIMES 0% FINANCING AND LARGE REBATES. THEN 2% FINANCING WAS A GOOD DEAL.

THE SIX OF US, MY WIFE AND FOUR CHILDREN, WENT OUT TO "BUY" A VAN! WE WENT OUT TO DINNER FIRST AND GOT "LAMBED UP." WE WERE ALL IN A GOOD MOOD, BECAUSE WE WERE GOING TO BUY A VAN THAT NIGHT AND GO TO DISNEY WORLD THE NEXT DAY.

WHEN WE GOT TO THE DEALERSHIP, THERE WERE LITERALLY HUNDREDS OF PEOPLE THERE, PROBABLY AS A DIRECT RESULT OF THEIR ADVERTISING.

WE WALKED AROUND FOR ABOUT 20 MINUTES AND CHOSE THE VAN WE WANTED TO BUY. IT WAS A CUSTOM VAN, WITH A SINK, TELEVISION, AND ALL THE FEATURES WE WANTED.

SHORTLY AFTER WE HAD CHOSEN THAT PARTICULAR VAN, A SALESPERSON CAME UP AND ASKED IF WE WERE WORKING WITH ANYONE. AFTER HEARING WE WEREN'T, HE APOLOGIZED FOR NO ONE BEING WITH US. HE WAS VERY CORDIAL.

HE ASKED IF WE WERE INTERESTED IN ACTUALLY PURCHASING A VAN THAT EVENING AND WE SAID, "YES!"

HE ASKED US IF WE HAD FOUND ANYTHING WE LIKED AND WE SAID, "YES, WE ARE STANDING IN FRONT OF IT."

# Bulls, Owls, Lambs and Tigers®: Personality Selling™

HE THEN SAID (PLEASE BELIEVE THIS, BECAUSE IT IS TRUE), "LET ME SHOW YOU SOME OF THE OTHER VANS." AND WE SAID, "OK."

AFTER HIM SHOWING HIS ENTIRE INVENTORY OF VANS, WE WERE STANDING IN FRONT OF THE VAN WE HAD ORIGINALLY CHOSEN AND HE SAID, "WHICH ONE DO YOU LIKE THE BEST, FOR YOUR NEEDS?" ALL SIX OF US SAID, "THIS ONE." (IT WAS THE ONE WE HAD CHOSEN IN THE BEGINNING.)

> **HE THEN SAID, "LET ME GO GET THE KEYS SO YOU CAN DRIVE IT."**

I TOLD THE SALESPERSON IT WOULDN'T BE NECESSARY, BECAUSE THE VAN WAS BRAND NEW, AND I HAD DRIVEN VANS LIKE THAT BEFORE. IT HAD A FULL WARRANTY.

HE SAID, "GOOD, BUT LET ME GO GET THE KEYS ANYWAY."

> **I SAID, "ACTUALLY ALL I WANT TO KNOW IS:**
>
> 1) **WHAT IS THE LOWEST PRICE AT WHICH I COULD BUY IT TONIGHT? (I DIDN'T WANT TO PAY STICKER PRICE.)**
>    **AND**
> 2) **WHAT IS THE LEAST AMOUNT FOR WHICH I COULD WRITE THE CHECK?"**

**I ASK YOU...WERE THOSE "BUYING SIGNS?"**

HE SAID (FOR THE 3ʳᴰ TIME), "I'LL GO GET THE KEYS," AND I SAID, "NO." HE REPLIED,

> **"YOU HAVE TO DRIVE IT FIRST, IT'S THE LAW!"**

I WAS STUNNED!

> I SAID, "IT'S NOT THE LAW," AND HE SAID, <u>"IT'S THE LAW OF OUR COMPANY, OR AT LEAST THE RULE</u>, THAT YOU HAVE TO DRIVE IT FIRST."

HE REALLY SAID THAT ("TRUE/TRUE.")

# Bulls, Owls, Lambs and Tigers®: Personality Selling™

I REMEMBER SAYING, "I WANT TO SEE YOUR SALES MANAGER," AND HE TOOK ME INTO A SALES MANAGER'S OFFICE. THAT WAS THE LAST I SAW OF THAT PARTICULAR SALESMAN.

AFTER WAITING IN THE SALES MANAGER'S OFFICE FOR ABOUT FIVE MINUTES (I DIDN'T TIME THAT ONE, I SHOULD HAVE), THE SALES MANAGER CAME IN AND WAS VERY PLEASANT. HE OFFERED MY CHILDREN QUARTERS FOR THE SODA POP MACHINE AND CANDY MACHINES. THREE OF THE FOUR TOOK HIM UP ON IT. I HAVE TWO SONS AND TWO DAUGHTERS: 1 BULL, 1 OWL, 1 LAMB AND 1 TIGER. WE WAITED ABOUT 10 MINUTES WHILE THE SALES MANAGER GOT MY CHILDREN "SQUARED AWAY" ON SNACKS.

(SEE, HE WAS OPERATING ON THE LIE/MYTH THAT IF YOU TAKE CARE OF THE CHILDREN FIRST, THE PARENTS WILL BE HAPPY.)

ALL I WANTED TO DO WAS TO BUY THE VAN THAT WE HAD SELECTED AND LEAVE WITH IT THAT NIGHT.

MY BULL DAUGHTER HAD ALREADY LEFT AND WALKED BACK TO THE CAR. AFTER MORE FOOLING AROUND, BY THE SALES MANAGER, MY OTHER THREE CHILDREN AND MY WIFE ALSO WENT BACK TO THE CAR.

> **HE FINALLY SAID TO ME, "WHAT CAN WE DO TONIGHT TO GET YOU INVOLVED WITH THE VAN YOU SELECTED?"**

I SAID, "WHAT THE SALESPERSON COULD HAVE DONE APPROXIMATELY 45 MINUTES AGO WAS TO TELL ME:

1) WHAT WAS THE LOWEST PRICE I COULD PAY FOR THE VAN?
AND
2) FOR HOW MUCH COULD I WRITE THE CHECK TONIGHT?

HE SAID, "I CAN ANSWER THAT."

I SAID, "I'M NOT INTERESTED NOW."

HE SAID, "SO, YOU ARE NOT GOING TO BUY TONIGHT?"

I SAID, "THAT'S RIGHT. I JUST WANTED TO SEE WHAT YOU WERE GOING TO DO NEXT." (MY SILENT VOICE SAID, HOW MUCH MORE WERE YOU GOING TO TORTURE ME AND MY FAMILY?)

WHAT HE SAID THEN, WILL SURPRISE YOU. (IT SURPRISED ME.) HE SAID, <u>"WE REALLY DIDN'T THINK YOU WERE A BUYER ANYWAY, BECAUSE YOU REFUSED TO DRIVE THE VAN."</u>

# Bulls, Owls, Lambs and Tigers®: Personality Selling™

I WAS SPEECHLESS AND JUST WALKED OUT, KEEPING MY TEMPER UNDER CONTROL.

YOUR THOUGHTS?

IT WAS THEIR OBJECTION, NOT MINE. THEY DIDN'T THINK I WAS A BUYER BECAUSE I WOULDN'T DRIVE THE VAN.

I HAVE DISCUSSED THIS WITH MANY DEALERSHIP OWNERS, MANAGERS AND SALESPEOPLE THROUGH THE YEARS, AND MOST OF THEM ARE CONVINCED THAT BY DRIVING THE VEHICLE FIRST, IT GETS THE PROSPECTIVE BUYER MORE EMOTIONALLY INVOLVED.

I (WE) DIDN'T WANT TO GET "EMOTIONALLY INVOLVED," AND DRIVE THE VAN. WE JUST WANTED TO BUY THE VAN (THAT NIGHT)!

ASK AROUND!

A GOOD 50%+ OF POTENTIAL BUYERS, DO NOT WANT TO DRIVE IT FIRST. (SOME DO. SOME DON'T!)

THE "RULE" OF THAT DEALERSHIP, "YOU'VE GOT TO DRIVE IT FIRST," THE SALESPERSON, AND THE SALES MANAGER GOT IN THE MIDDLE OF THE CLARKE FAMILY AND THAT VAN, AND MADE IT SO WE DIDN'T BUY IT.

**P.S. THAT DEALERSHIP IN ST. PETERSBURG, FLORIDA IS NO LONGER IN BUSINESS. THEY DROVE THEMSELVES OUT OF BUSINESS, WITH THEIR OWN "LIES AND MYTHS" IN SELLING.**

THIS EXPERIENCE WAS A FIVE ON THE FIVE-TO-ONE "TORTURE SCALE" FOR MY FAMILY AND ME.

# Bulls, Owls, Lambs and Tigers®: Personality Selling™

> **EXAMPLE #2**
>
> **SELLING NEW CADILLACS**
>
> **VINNY, "YO LET'S DO IT!"**

LET'S CONTRAST THE LAST STORY TO WHEN I WAS IN THE PHILADELPHIA AREA.

I HAD DONE AN ALL-DAY SEMINAR AND JUST WANTED TO GO TO THE BRAND-NEW CADILLAC DEALERSHIP TO SEE THE BRAND-NEW CADILLAC, THAT HAD JUST COME OUT.

I WAS IN THE SHOWROOM SITTING IN THE BRAND-NEW CADILLAC WITH THE DOOR OPEN AND THE WINDOW DOWN, WHEN THE SALESPERSON CAME UP AND INTRODUCED HIMSELF, "YO, I'M VINNY. HOW YA DOING?" (HE LOOKED LIKE JOE PESCI, OUT OF "MY COUSIN VINNY.")

HE ASKED ME MY NAME AND I SAID I WAS CHARLES CLARKE III (AS I ALWAYS DO) AND HE SAID, "YO, MR. CHARLIE. HOW DO YOU LIKE THIS CADILLAC?" I SAID, "I LOVE IT!"

> **HE SAID,**
>
> **"YO, LET'S DO IT!"**

THIS WAS AFTER ABOUT 30 SECONDS TOGETHER.

DO YOU THINK HIS BEHAVIOR WAS TOO PUSHY? (I DIDN'T.)

AFTER HE SAID THE ABOVE, I RESPONDED AND SAID, "NO." (I WAS NOW STANDING UP OUTSIDE THE CAR.)

HE SAID, "YO, WHY NOT?" (EVERYTHING STARTED OR ENDED WITH A "YO," WITH HIM.)

I SAID, "I LIVE IN TAMPA, FLORIDA (WHERE I LIVED AT THE TIME)."

HE SAID, "YO, WE SHIP."

I SAID, "NO, IF I WERE REALLY INTERESTED IN BUYING A BRAND-NEW CADILLAC, I WOULD BUY IT IN TAMPA."

# Bulls, Owls, Lambs and Tigers®: Personality Selling™

### HIS RESPONSE

"YO, I UNDERSTAND. YOU HAVE CONVINCED ME YOU ARE NOT BUYING FROM ME TODAY. IS THERE ANY CHANCE OF YOU EVER BUYING FROM ME, NEXT MONTH, NEXT YEAR, OR TWO YEARS FROM NOW?"

I SAID, "NO, VINNY. YOU WILL PROBABLY NEVER SEE ME AGAIN, BUT I CAN TELL YOU ARE AN EXCELLENT SALESPERSON." HE SAID, "YO, HAVE A NICE DAY."

I "STALKED" HIM ON THAT CROWDED NIGHT AND HEARD HIM DELIVER THE SAME MESSAGE TO SEVERAL PEOPLE OR COUPLES. "DO YOU LIKE IT?" AND "YO, LET'S DO IT!"

ONE COUPLE SAID THEY DIDN'T LIKE A PARTICULAR CAR AND HE POINTED TO ANOTHER ONE AND THEY SAID THEY LIKED THAT ONE AND HE SAID,

> "YO, LET'S DO IT!"

THE MAN FROM THE COUPLE SAID, "WELL, YOU WOULD REALLY HAVE TO SHARPEN YOUR PENCIL," AND VINNY SAID ONE OF THE CORNIEST THINGS I HAVE EVER HEARD. VINNY REPLIED, "YO, I JUST GOT A BRAND-NEW PENCIL SHARPENER. COME ON IN TO MY OFFICE, YO."

I WAS HEADING TO BUDAPEST, HUNGARY, THE NEXT DAY ON BUSINESS AND DIDN'T HAVE TIME TO WAIT AROUND TO SEE IF HE CLOSED THEM, SO I ASKED THE SALES MANAGER IF I COULD CALL HIM LATER TO SEE IF VINNY HAD "CLOSED" THEM.

THE SALES MANAGER SAID, "COME, LET ME SHOW YOU SOMETHING." HE SHOWED ME VINNY'S "WALL OF PLAQUES." VINNY WAS THE #1 SALESPERSON FOR THAT COMPANY IN NEW CADILLAC SALES AND WAS TOP SALESPERSON FOR THAT ENTIRE AREA.

> LET ME ASK YOU THIS. IF VINNY HAD BEEN SELLING VANS WHEN I WAS TRYING TO BUY A VAN, DO YOU THINK HE WOULD HAVE SOLD ME? THE ANSWER IS YES (AND QUICKLY)!

> THE VAN SALESPERSON, MANAGER AND THE ENTIRE COMPANY HAD "LIES AND MYTHS" AS THEIR DOCTRINE. VINNY DID NOT.

YOUR THOUGHTS?

> YO, LET'S DO IT!

# NOTES

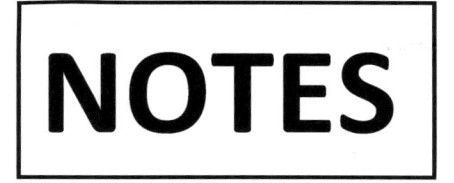

THINGS I AGREE WITH

THINGS I DISAGREE WITH

THINGS I NEED TO WORK ON

ACTION PLAN FOR ME

## CHAPTER 33

> **LIE/MYTH #30: IN SELLING AT SHOWS AND CONVENTIONS, THE MOST IMPORTANT THING A SALESPERSON CAN DO, RIGHT AWAY, IS TO TELL A LITTLE ABOUT THEIR COMPANY.**

DO AN EXPERIMENT ON YOUR OWN THE NEXT TIME YOU ARE AT A CONVENTION, AND COMPANIES ARE DISPLAYING THEIR WARES.

WALK UP TO DIFFERENT BOOTHS AND SEE WHAT THEY SAY AND DO. THEY WILL SAY:

> **"ARE YOU FAMILIAR WITH OUR COMPANY?"**

IF THE ANSWER IS NO, THEY START A "WIND UP" PRESENTATION ON THEIR COMPANY, AND START **"FEATURE DUMPING,"** TELLING YOU EVERYTHING ABOUT THEIR COMPANY AND PRODUCT (ALL WITHIN A FEW MINUTES).

RIGHT?

CERTAINLY, YOU HAVE EXPERIENCED THE ABOVE.

WHAT SHOULD THEY BE DOING IN THAT FEW MINUTES OF VALUABLE TIME? THEY SHOULD "QUALIFY/QUALIFY/QUALIFY (READY, WILLING AND ABLE)," INSTEAD OF TELLING OR SELLING.

**READY** – "ARE YOU IN THE MARKET FOR THIS?" "WHEN MIGHT YOU OR THE COMPANY BE PURCHASING?"

**WILLING** – "WHAT ARE YOUR NEEDS?"

**ABLE** – "WHAT IS YOUR PRICE RANGE?"

THEN, IF A PERSON IS A 3 GREEN DOT PROSPECT, GET THEIR BUSINESS CARD AND INFORMATION, AND SET A POSSIBLE APPOINTMENT OR PHONE APPOINTMENT. YOU CAN DO THAT IN LESS THAN THREE MINUTES, INSTEAD OF" FEATURE DUMPING."

# Bulls, Owls, Lambs and Tigers®: Personality Selling™

> **"HUNGRY. WANNA EAT?"**

I WAS SPEAKING AT A HOUSTON CONVENTION THAT HAD ABOUT 90,000 TOTAL ATTENDEES. AT LUNCH TIME, I NOTICED A LUNCH TENT THAT WAS SET BACK ABOUT 40 YARDS OFF THE BEATEN PATH. IT LOOKED LIKE IT COULD HOLD ABOUT 1000 PEOPLE AND THERE WERE ONLY ABOUT 20 TO 30 PEOPLE HAVING LUNCH IN THERE. MOST ALL THE OTHER LUNCH TENTS WERE COMPLETELY FULL.

I ASKED TO SEE THE MANAGER AND MADE A FINANCIAL DEAL WITH HIM, BASED SOLELY ON THE <u>INCREASE</u> OF THOSE EATING THERE.

I SUGGESTED HE IMMEDIATELY MAKE SIGNS THAT SAID, "HUNGRY, WANNA EAT?" I ALSO SUGGESTED HIM HAVING TEN OF THE EMPLOYEES, WHO WEREN'T REALLY DOING ANYTHING, GO OUT AND HOLD UP THE SIGNS. I INSTRUCTED HIM TO HAVE THE EMPLOYEES ALSO ASK PEOPLE AS THEY WERE PASSING BY, "ARE YOU HUNGRY?"

IF THEY SAID, "YES," THE EMPLOYEES WERE TO REPLY, "DO YOU WANNA EAT? IF YES, COME ON IN FOR THE BEST RIBS AND BARBEQUE."

IN NO TIME, THE ENTIRE TENT WAS FULL.

> **ASK FOR THE CLOSE!**

> **WHATEVER YOU ARE SELLING!**

# NOTES

THINGS I AGREE WITH

THINGS I DISAGREE WITH

THINGS I NEED TO WORK ON

ACTION PLAN FOR ME

# CHAPTER 34

> **LIE/MYTH #31: IN SELLING, IF YOU WERE SELLING EXPENSIVE MEN'S SUITS, IT WOULD BE TOO PUSHY TO TRY TO CLOSE A PROSPECT, VERSUS LETTING THEM DECIDE ON THEIR OWN.**

### UPPER STATE NEW YORK SUIT STORY

I WAS CONSULTING WITH A COMPANY IN UPPER STATE NEW YORK AND FRANK HAD TO SEE HIS ATTORNEY IN THE DOWNTOWN AREA. INSTEAD OF GOING UP TO THE WAITING ROOM OF THE ATTORNEY'S OFFICE, I CHOSE TO GO ACROSS THE STREET TO A MEN'S CLOTHING STORE THAT HAD A SIGN SAYING, "$1,000 SUITS FOR $300 - MOVING TO THE SUBURBS SALES."

I WENT IN AND SAID I WAS, "JUST LOOKING." THE SALESPERSON ASKED IF I WOULD LIKE TO TRY ON SOME SUITS, IN MY SIZE, AND I SAID, "YES."

I HAD ALREADY TOLD THE SALESPERSON THAT I ONLY HAD TWENTY MINUTES. I TRIED ON FIVE SUIT JACKETS, (THE LAST ONE OF THEM WAS AN ARMANI.) I ALSO TRIED ON THE PANTS OF THE ARMANI.

THE SALESPERSON ASKED ME,

1) "HOW DO YOU LIKE OUR SUITS?" AND
2) "WHICH ONE, OR ONES, DO YOU LIKE THE BEST?"

I RESPONDED BY SAYING THAT I LIKED THE ARMANI THE BEST, BUT I ALSO LIKED TWO OF THE OTHER SUITS.

THE SALESPERON SAID SOMETHING LIKE, "I KNOW, YOU ONLY HAD 20 MINUTES WHICH WE ALREADY HAVE USED UP. I'M WONDERING IF YOU WOULD BE ABLE TO COME BACK AT 6:00PM, WHEN YOU WOULD HAVE MORE TIME?"

HE WENT ON TO SAY THAT HE WOULD PUT THE THREE SUITS I LIKED, ON HOLD UNTIL 6:00PM, WHEN I HAD EXPRESSED THAT I COULD POSSIBLY COME BACK. I SAID THAT I WOULD BE ABLE TO COME BACK THEN AND THAT I APPRECIATED HIM DOING THAT.

BEFORE YOU GO ON AND READ MORE, WHAT WERE <u>YOUR</u> THOUGHTS ON THE SALESPERSON?

# Bulls, Owls, Lambs and Tigers®: Personality Selling™

WRITE DOWN YOUR THOUGHTS, BEFORE READING ON:

_____

_____

WHEN I ASK THIS QUESTION IN MY SEMINARS, I USUALLY GET ANSWERS LIKE, "HE WAS REALLY GOOD," "HE WAS EXCELLENT AT CUSTOMER SERVICE," AND "HE WAS NOT TOO PUSHY, AND VERY ACCOMMODATING."

LET ME TELL YOU WHAT HAPPENED. I DID NOT GO BACK AT 6:00PM. I REALLY INTENDED TO DO SO, BUT I DIDN'T, BECAUSE SOMETHING GOT IN THE WAY. I DON'T KNOW WHAT IT WAS EXCEPT FOR SAYING THAT IT WAS "LIFE!"

I NEVER WENT BACK AND I DID NOT BUY THE SUITS.

I WAS ON A PLANE BACK HOME AT ABOUT 11PM AND IT WAS THE FIRST TIME SINCE I WAS IN THE STORE THAT I THOUGHT ABOUT THE SUITS.

I STARTED THINKING WHAT COULD HAVE HAPPENED DIFFERENTLY FOR ME TO HAVE BOUGHT THE SUITS. THE SALESPERSON COULD HAVE SAID,

1) "CHARLES, HOW DO YOU LIKE OUR SUITS?"
2) "WHICH ONE OR ONES DO YOU LIKE THE BEST?"
3) **"WHAT DO YOU THINK ABOUT GOING AHEAD WITH THIS TODAY?"**

I KNOW WHAT I WOULD HAVE SAID. I WOULD HAVE SAID, "NO" AND I MIGHT HAVE EVEN BEEN A BIT IRRITATED BECAUSE I HAD ALREADY TOLD HIM I WAS ON A SHORT TIME-FRAME.

HE THEN COULD HAVE SAID, "I UNDERSTAND, BUT I'M CONCERNED IF YOU DON'T BUY THE THREE SUITS NOW, YOU MIGHT NEVER COME BACK. YOU COULD BUY $3,000+ WORTH OF SUITS FOR $900. I SUGGEST YOU GIVE ME YOUR CREDIT CARD AND I'LL HAVE ALL THREE SUITS RUNG UP, AND READY FOR YOU, BY THE TIME YOU GET THOSE ARMANI SUIT PANTS OFF, AND BACK ON THE HANGER."

I WOULD HAVE BOUGHT ALL THREE SUITS!

I'M STILL WHINING AND COMPLAINING ABOUT NOT HAVING BOUGHT THOSE THREE, BEAUTIFUL SUITS, FOR THAT PRICE.

WHO LOST OUT ON THAT?

I LOST OUT, THE SALESPERSON, AND THE STORE OWNER LOST OUT.

**Bulls, Owls, Lambs and Tigers®: Personality Selling™**

> **HE DIDN'T EVEN ASK IF I WANTED TO PURCHASE. HE JUST SET THE APPOINTMENT FOR ME TO COME BACK.**

HAVE YOU EVER DONE THAT? HOW OFTEN? WHEN WAS THE LAST TIME YOU SET AN APPOINTMENT WITHOUT ASKING THEM IF THEY WOULD GO AHEAD WITH THIS TODAY?

IF YOU HAD ANSWERED THAT YOU THOUGHT HE WAS A GOOD SALESPERSON, I WANT YOU TO "RE-THINK" YOUR ANSWER.

HE WAS NOT A GOOD SALESPERSON. HE WAS A PLEASANT SALESPERSON, BUT NOT EVEN "GOOD." HE DID NOT EVEN MAKE AN ATTEMPT TO CLOSE. JUST AN ORDER TAKER.

YOUR THOUGHTS?

**CONTRAST STORY**

LAST DECEMBER I WENT INTO A MEN'S CLOTHING STORE IN JOHNSON CITY, TENNESSEE. THE NIGHT BEFORE, MY WIFE, ANNE, AND I WERE AT A PARTY IN KINGSPORT, TENNESSEE, (HOME OF EASTMAN CHEMICAL COMPANY) WHERE I COMPLIMENTED A PROMINENT ATTORNEY, WAYNE, ON HIS EXQUISITE SUIT. (HE'S A "FASHION PLATE".) I ASKED HIM WHERE HE BOUGHT IT AND HE TOLD ME WM KING CLOTHIERS, IN JOHNSON CITY (CLOSE BY). WE WENT THERE THE NEXT MORNING JUST TO SEE SOME OF THE OTHER "ONE-OF-A-KIND" SUITS (WOOL AND CASHMERE BLEND SUITS AND UNUSUAL PATTERNS OF CLOTH).

I TRIED ON A COUPLE SUITS AND REALLY LIKED ONE PARTICULAR, EXPENSIVE SUIT.

I REALLY HAD NO INTENTION OF BUYING A SUIT THAT DAY. WE JUST HAD NOTHING ELSE TO DO THAT MORNING AND WANTED TO SEE THIS EXCLUSIVE MEN'S CLOTHING STORE.

AS I WAS GETTING READY TO TAKE THE SUIT OFF AND LEAVE, THE SALES MANAGER, ROGER, WHO WAS ALSO MY SALESPERSON SAID TO ME,

> **"I AM GOING TO SELL YOU THIS SUIT TODAY."**

I TRULY THOUGHT HIS STATEMENT WAS A LITTLE "BOLD."

© 2021 Charles J. Clarke III. "Bulls, Owls, Lambs and Tigers®" is a registered federal trademark of Charles J. Clarke III since 1988. Personality Selling™ and BOLT™ are Trademarks of Charles J. Clarke III. NO reproduction in any form is allowed.

HE CONTINUED, "THERE IS NO REASON FOR YOU **NOT** TO BUY THIS SUIT. YOU LOOK LIKE A MILLION BUCKS IN IT. IT FITS YOU PERFECTLY. YOU'RE NOT LEAVING, WITHOUT BUYING IT."

I SAID, "OK."

IF HE HAD NOT CLOSED ME THAT DAY, I WOULD HAVE NEVER GONE BACK. NOW I WILL RETURN MANY TIMES, WHEN I AM BACK IN THE AREA.

**WHICH APPROACH DO YOU LIKE BEST?**

WHO MADE THE SALE?

IT'S MY FAVORITE SUIT. (THANK YOU, ROGER!)

YOUR THOUGHTS?

# NOTES

THINGS I AGREE WITH

THINGS I DISAGREE WITH

THINGS I NEED TO WORK ON

ACTION PLAN FOR ME

# CHAPTER 35

> # LIE/MYTH #32: IN SELLING WE HAVE TO ALWAYS BE LOOKING FOR BUYING SIGNS AND ACT UPON THOSE SIGNS.

> **BE CAREFUL OF THIS ONE, BECAUSE WE OFTEN LOOK FOR THE SIGNS <u>WE</u> WOULD SHOW IF WE WERE THE BUYER.**

LOOK AT ONE OF THE LAST EXAMPLES ABOUT THE VAN STORY IN CHAPTER 32, MYTH #29. THE SALESPERSON OBVIOUSLY DID <u>NOT</u> SEE MY "BUYING SIGNS," ("WHAT'S YOUR LOWEST PRICE?" AND "FOR HOW MUCH COULD I WRITE THE CHECK?") BECAUSE THAT'S NOT WHAT HE WOULD HAVE DONE, IF HE HAD <u>NOT</u> CHOSEN TO "DRIVE THE VAN."

"DRIVING" THE VAN WOULD HAVE BEEN <u>HIS</u> BUYING SIGN, AND IF HE, AS A BUYER, WOULD HAVE CHOSEN NOT TO DRIVE THE VAN, THEN THAT WOULD HAVE BEEN A "NON-BUYING," SIGN. NOTHING ELSE WOULD HAVE MATTERED. DOES THIS MAKE SENSE?

### EXAMPLE #2

YOU, AS A SALESPERSON, ASK THE POTENTIAL BUYER HOW HE/SHE LIKES THE PRODUCT. IF YOU ARE A TIGER/LAMB, YOU SHOW A LOT OF EMOTION. YOU WOULD EXPECT IF SOMEONE LIKED SOMETHING, THEY ALSO WOULD SHOW A LOT OF EMOTION (NOT ALWAYS TRUE), OR AS WE DISCUSSED EARLIER, OWLS BUY WITH LOGIC AND JUSTIFY WITH LOGIC (HOMES, CARS, EVERYTHING).

IF <u>YOU</u> ASK AN OWL HOW <u>THEY</u> LIKE THE CAR OR HOME THEY MIGHT SAY, "IT'S OK," WITHOUT <u>SHOWING</u> ANY EMOTION. THEY THEN MIGHT ASK A TECHNICAL QUESTION INSTEAD OF SHOWING EMOTION AND YOUR TIGER/LAMB INTERPRETATION OF THEIR "OK" IS THAT THEY <u>DIDN'T</u> LIKE IT.

AGAIN, MY POINT IS, SOMETIMES A BUYER DOES NOT SHOW THE SIGNS <u>YOU</u> WOULD SHOW. THUS, YOU <u>MISINTERPRET</u> THEIR BUYING SIGN (JUST LIKE THE <u>VAN SALESPERSON</u>), AND LOSE THE SALE.

# Bulls, Owls, Lambs and Tigers®: Personality Selling™

## EXAMPLE #3

A BULL IS IN THEIR "BULL-MODE BODY LANGUAGE POSITION (TIGHT BODY LANGUAGE AND NO SMILE)," WHILE ASKING FOR A BETTER PRICE, THAT IS ALREADY A BUYING SIGN FOR THE BULL. YET, YOU MIGHT NOT INTERPRET IT THAT WAY AND YOU MAY LOSE THE SALE.

WORK ON UNDERSTANDING BUYING SIGNS FOR EACH PERSONALITY, BECAUSE IT IS SO IMPORTANT.

> THE MORE OWL/BULLS LIKE SOMETHING, THE LESS THEY SHOW EMOTION.

> THE MORE TIGER/LAMBS LIKE SOMETHING, THE MORE THEY SHOW EMOTION.

TIGER/LAMBS REALLY HAVE A HARD TIME WITH READING OWL/BULL BUYING SIGNS, AND VICE VERSA.

> HAVE YOU HAD AN "EPIPHANY" (SUDDEN AWAKENING TO A TRUTH) YET?

WITH WHICH CHAPTER DID YOU START HAVING AN EPIPHANY?

# NOTES

THINGS I AGREE WITH

THINGS I DISAGREE WITH

THINGS I NEED TO WORK ON

ACTION PLAN FOR ME

# CHAPTER 36

## LIE/MYTH #33: SELLING INTANGIBLES (SOMETHING YOU CAN'T SEE OR TOUCH) IS HARDER THAN SELLING TANGIBLES.

IT'S NOT REALLY HARDER, IT'S JUST DIFFERENT.

**EXAMPLE 1**

WHICH ANIMAL PERSONALITY DO YOU THINK HAS THE EASIEST TIME OF READING BLUEPRINTS AND FLOOR PLANS? WHOSE BRAIN HAS A HARDER TIME INTERPRETING BLUEPRINTS AND FLOOR PLANS?

IT GOES IN THIS ORDER, FROM EASIEST TO HARDEST:

OWLS   #1      EASIEST TIME

BULLS  #2      2ND EASIEST TIME

LAMBS  #3      2ND HARDEST TIME

TIGERS #4      HARDEST TIME

BUYING OFF A FLOOR PLAN OR OFF A BLUEPRINT (BEFORE THERE IS A MODEL) IS MORE OF BUYING AN "INTANGIBLE", BECAUSE THEY CAN NOT SEE IT.

**IN THE NEW HOME SELLING ARENA, OWLS AND BULLS (IN THAT ORDER) HAVE A HIGHER PROBABILITY OF BUYING "PRE-SALES."**

TIGERS AND LAMBS SAY THEY HAVE TO "SEE A MODEL FIRST," OR A HOME LIKE IT, THAT HAS ALREADY BEEN BUILT.

IF A SALESPERSON IS A TIGER/LAMB THEY THINK <u>EVERYONE</u> NEEDS TO SEE A MODEL FIRST, WHICH IS ONLY ABOUT 50% CORRECT.

# Bulls, Owls, Lambs and Tigers®: Personality Selling™

---

**EXAMPLE TWO**

**SELLING "FRANCHISES," BEFORE THEY ARE PROVEN**

---

IMAGINE HOW TOUGH IT WOULD HAVE BEEN TO SELL THE FIRST OR THE FIRST 100 MCDONALD'S FRANCHISES, OR ANY OTHER NEW FRANCHISE. NOW THERE ARE OVER 34,000 MCDONALD'S FRANCHISES AND IT'S AN EASY SALE IF SOMEONE HAS THE LARGE AMOUNT OF MONEY TO PURCHASE ONE.

THE FIRST INVESTOR OBVIOUSLY DID NOT HAVE TO PAY AS MUCH, BECAUSE THEY WERE "BUYING A DREAM," WHICH HAD NOT YET MATERIALIZED.

**TODAY'S AMERICAN BUILDER**

I WAS ON THE GROUND FLOOR OF A FRANCHISE CALLED, "TODAY'S AMERICAN BUILDER." IT WAS A FRANCHISE OUT OF HOUSTON, TEXAS, FOR SMALLER VOLUME BUILDERS, MUCH LIKE THE FRANCHISES FOR REALTORS® THAT HAD ALREADY BEEN ESTABLISHED.

THE REGIONAL DIRECTOR OF CENTURY 21'S REGION OF TEXAS AND LOUISIANA, ERNIE FITZPATRICK, STARTED TODAY'S AMERICAN BUILDER. I HAD BEEN HIS FIRST VICE PRESIDENT OF CENTURY 21'S REGION OF TEXAS AND LOUISIANA, AND LATER BECAME THE NATIONAL TRAINING DIRECTOR FOR TODAY'S AMERICAN BUILDER.

LATER MY FAMILY AND I MOVED TO FLORIDA, WHERE I BECAME PRESIDENT AND REGIONAL DIRECTOR OF THE FLORIDA DIVISION.

IN A VERY SHORT PERIOD OF TIME (APPROXIMATELY 2 YEARS) TODAY'S AMERICAN BUILDER HAD SOLD APPROXIMATELY 14 MASTER FRANCHISES (REGIONAL TERRITORIES SUCH AS THE STATE OF FLORIDA, STATE OF CALIFORNIA, THE CAROLINAS, DALLAS, HOUSTON, ETC).

WE HAD SOLD ALL ACROSS THE UNITED STATES, AND SOME OF THE MASTER FRANCHISES WERE SEVERAL HUNDRED THOUSAND OF DOLLARS.

WE SOLD OVER 200 INDIVIDUAL FRANCHISES IN THAT SAME PERIOD OF TIME (EACH SELLING FOR ABOUT $7,000 TO $12,000).

THAT IS A TOUGH SALE! (DIFFERENT, BUT TOUGH) BECAUSE IT HAD NOT YET BEEN "PROVEN."

# Bulls, Owls, Lambs and Tigers®: Personality Selling™

WE WERE SELLING A "FUTURE DREAM," THAT WAS NOT IN PLACE YET. BUYERS WERE GETTING IN ON THE "GROUND FLOOR" THAT "PROMISED:"

1) <u>KNOWLEDGE, EDUCATION AND RESEARCH</u> (THAT THE LARGER BUILDERS HAD, BUT SMALLER BUILDERS DID NOT HAVE),
2) <u>NATIONAL RECOGNITION</u> AND NATIONAL ADVERTISING AS A CONGLOMERATE, THAT INDIVIDUAL BUILDERS DID NOT HAVE
3) <u>BUYING POWER</u>, AS A CONGLOMERATE, THAT INDIVIDUAL SMALLER BUILDERS DID NOT HAVE.

AS THE REGIONAL DIRECTOR AND PRESIDENT OF THE FLORIDA DIVISION, OUR TEAM AND I SOLD OVER 20 INDIVIDUAL FRANCHISES IN JUST A LITTLE OVER ONE YEAR.

**THE FIRST POINT**

WHO WERE THE BUYERS?

AS POINTED OUT, OWLS AND BULLS HAVE A HIGHER PROBABILITY OF BUYING SOMETHING THEY CAN'T SEE, BUT BULLS AND TIGERS ARE THE HIGHER RISK TAKERS. SO, WHO WERE THE <u>MASTER FRANCHISE</u> BUYERS AND WHO BOUGHT THE INDIVIDUAL FRANCHISES?

<u>ANSWER:</u>

BULL/OWLS

AND

BULL/TIGERS

MOST FRANCHISES THAT ARE SOLD IN THE BEGINNING, BEFORE EVERYTHING IS ESTABLISHED, ARE THOSE SAME PERSONALITIES.

**THE SECOND POINT**

BEFORE YOU START SELLING, YOU REALLY NEED TO KNOW WHO YOUR BUYER IS FOR A PARTICULAR PRODUCT. YOU ALSO REALLY NEED TO BELIEVE IN THE PRODUCT (DREAM) YOURSELF!

© 2021 Charles J. Clarke III. "Bulls, Owls, Lambs and Tigers®" is a registered federal trademark of Charles J. Clarke III since 1988. Personality Selling™ and BOLT™ are Trademarks of Charles J. Clarke III. NO reproduction in any form is allowed.

# Bulls, Owls, Lambs and Tigers®: Personality Selling™

## THE REST OF THE STORY

THE VENTURE WAS UNDERCAPITALIZED AND GREW TOO FAST IN ORDER TO PROVIDE THE SERVICES.

EVENTUALLY ALL THE REGIONS, EXCEPT FOR OUR FLORIDA REGION, SLOWLY VANISHED, AND IT WAS HARD TO KEEP THE FLORIDA REGION GOING WITHOUT THE REST OF THE NATION'S SUPPORT. THAT IS WHEN I FORMED CHARLES CLARKE CONSULTING, INC. WHICH PROVIDED MANY OF THE SERVICES THAT TODAY'S AMERICAN BUILDERS HAD PROVIDED, IN THE AREA OF KNOWLEDGE, EDUCATION AND RESEARCH.

TODAY'S AMERICAN BUILDER WAS ACTUALLY A CONCEPT "AHEAD OF ITS TIME," (LIKE MANY FRANCHISES AND VENTURES).

MOST EVERYBODY MADE MONEY WAY BEYOND THEIR INITIAL INVESTMENT, BUT NOT WHAT THEY "IMAGINED" THEY COULD ACHIEVE.

IN SELLING "INTANGIBLES" YOU REALLY HAVE TO BE ABLE TO "SELLTHE DREAM" AND GET INSIDE THEIR OWN "DREAM MACHINE," AS WELL AS YOURS.

> HAVE YOU SEEN THE HISTORY CHANNEL'S "THE MEN WHO BUILT AMERICA?" (YOU SHOULD.) IT WAS ABOUT THE GIANTS: CARNEGIE, VANDERBILT, ROCKEFELLER, MORGAN, EDISON, ETC., WHO HAD A "DREAM"AND HAD TO **SELL** IT TO OTHERS.

## THAT'S SELLING INTANGIBLES!

EVEN IF YOU DON'T SELL INTANGIBLES, OR NEVER WILL, THESE ARE LESSONS TO BE LEARNING.

WHAT DID YOU GAIN FROM THAT EXAMPLE OF SELLING INTANGIBLES?

# NOTES

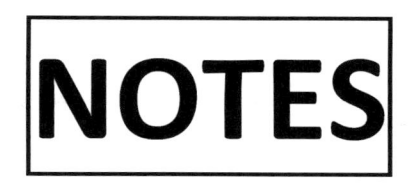

THINGS I AGREE WITH

THINGS I DISAGREE WITH

THINGS I NEED TO WORK ON

ACTION PLAN FOR ME

# Bulls, Owls, Lambs and Tigers®: Personality Selling™

## CHAPTER 37

> # LIE/MYTH #34: IN "RESTAURANT SELLING," A WAITER OR WAITRESS SHOULD ALWAYS TELL ABOUT THE RESTAURANT SPECIALS (IF THEY HAVE SPECIALS).

SOME PEOPLE DON'T SEE CUSTOMER SERVICE IN A RESTAURANT, HOTEL, OR SERVICE INDUSTRY, AS "SELLING," BUT IT CERTAINLY IS.

MY GOOD FRIEND, JOE BRACCIALE FROM FLORIDA, WHO IS A BULL, CAN TELL YOU ABOUT THIS. ONE OF HIS PET PEEVES IS WHEN A WAITER OR WAITRESS, IN AN EXCELLENT RESTAURANT OR ANY RESTAURANT, SAYS, "LET ME TELL YOU ABOUT TONIGHT'S SPECIALS."

HE SOMETIMES LET'S THEM GO ON AND ON JUST TO SEE HOW "RIDICULOUS" THEY ARE.

AFTER THEY HAVE "BURIED" THEMSELVES WITH HIM AND "TORTURED" HIM, HE SAYS, "I WANT A STEAK, MEDIUM RARE, AND THAT'S WHAT I WANTED WHEN I FIRST WALKED IN, BEFORE YOU DECIDED TO "**TORTURE**" ME WITH YOUR SPECIALS!" IT REALLY MAKES HIM MAD, AND HE REALLY SAYS THAT.

I'M SUGGESTING THEY ARE "TORTURING" A GOOD 50% OF THEIR PATRONS. WHAT SHOULD THE WAITERS AND WAITRESS DO INSTEAD?

ASK, "WOULD YOU LIKE TO HEAR TONIGHT'S SPEACIALS?"

JOE WOULD SAY, "NO, I WANT A STEAK (NAMING THE STEAK), MEDIUM RARE."

> **MORE RESTAURANT TORTURE SYSTEMS**

**EXAMPLE 1:** WAITER OR WAITRESS SAYS, "MY FAVORITE DISH TONIGHT IS _____ ." (BULLS AND SOME OTHERS ARE THINKING, "WHO CARES?")

**EXAMPLE 2:** THE MANAGER, WHOM YOU HAVEN'T SEEN ALL NIGHT, COMES UP TO YOU AT THE END OF YOUR MEAL, INTERRUPTS YOUR CONVERSATION, AND SAYS, "HOW IS EVERYTHING?"

**EXAMPLE 3:** THE HOSTESS (AT THE HOSTESS STATION) ASKS YOU AND YOUR SPOUSE "WILL THAT BE TWO FOR DINNER?" (SOME BULLS ARE THINKING, INNER VOICE "NO, THAT WILL BE TEN FOR BOWLING.")

**EXAMPLE 4:** WAITER OR WAITRESS KEEPS COMING TO YOUR TABLE AS YOU ARE EATING AND TALKING, (INTERRUPTING) TO MAKE SURE EVERYTHING IS OK.

# Bulls, Owls, Lambs and Tigers®: Personality Selling™

SEND ME SOME OF YOUR FAVORITE EXAMPLES OF TORTURE SYSTEMS USED IN THE SERVICE INDUSTRY.

---

**TORTURE AT MY BANK**

**(I'LL KEEP THEIR NAME ANONYMOUS)**

---

"HOW ARE YOU TODAY?" "HOW IS YOUR DAY?" (EVEN WHEN I'M IN A HURRY AND DON'T WANT TO EXPLAIN)

"HOW MAY WE BE OF SERVICE TO YOU TODAY?" (AS I'M JUST HEADING TOWARD THE TELLER WINDOW LIKE I ALWAYS DO, TRYING TO AVOID THE OVER-FRIENDLY "INSINCERE" GREETER)

---

I HAVE TO NOW GO IN THE BACK DOOR, TO AVOID, WHEN SHE ASKS, "HOW MAY I HELP YOU?" ON SOME DAYS, <u>MY INNER VOICE</u> SAYS, "YOU CAN HELP ME BY LEAVING ME ALONE TODAY AND QUIT "TORTURING" ME EVERY TIME I COME IN, WHEN I'M OBVIOUSLY IN A HURRY!" THIS IS ONLY "MILD TORTURE," IN THE "NAME OF CUSTOMER SERVICE." IF YOU ARE WONDERING WHY I'M STILL WITH THEM, I JUST HAVEN'T TAKEN TIME TO SWITCH BANKS. I WILL!

---

**TORTURE AT HOTELS (SOME HAVE THREE GREETERS AS YOU WALK INTO THE EXPENSIVE HOTELS)**

---

IT'S AS IF YOU HAVE TO GO THROUGH THE "GAUNTLET" TO ARRIVE AT THE FRONT DESK.

**FIRST ONE SAYS**, "HOW ARE YOU TODAY?"

**SECOND ONE SAYS**, "WE HOPE YOU HAD A PLEASANT DAY."

**THIRD ONE SAYS**, "LET US KNOW HOW WE CAN MAKE YOUR STAY MORE PLEASANT."

THEN THE BELLMAN "GETS YOU" LATER ON THE ELEVATOR.

SOMETIMES, <u>MY INNER VOICE</u> SAYS, "LEAVE ME ALONE!"

---

© 2021 Charles J. Clarke III. "Bulls, Owls, Lambs and Tigers®" is a registered federal trademark of Charles J. Clarke III since 1988. Personality Selling™ and BOLT™ are Trademarks of Charles J. Clarke III. NO reproduction in any form is allowed.

# Bulls, Owls, Lambs and Tigers®: Personality Selling™

> **SOME PLACES DO IT RIGHT; SOME DO IT WRONG.**

*THE RITZ CARLTON DID IT BEST!*

> **SELLING IS SELLING**

EVEN AT A FAST-FOOD RESTAURANT, THE VOICE OVER THE SPEAKER CAN BE VERY ANNOYING. AFTER YOUR ORDER:

"A CHEESEBURGER AND THAT WILL BE ALL."

THE VOICE SAYS, "WOULD YOU LIKE FRIES WITH THAT?"

YOU REPLY, "NO, THAT WILL BE <u>ALL</u>!"

THE VOICE SAYS, "HOW ABOUT A COLA?"

YOU REPLY, "NO, THAT WILL BE <u>ALL</u>!"

YOU GET THE POINT!

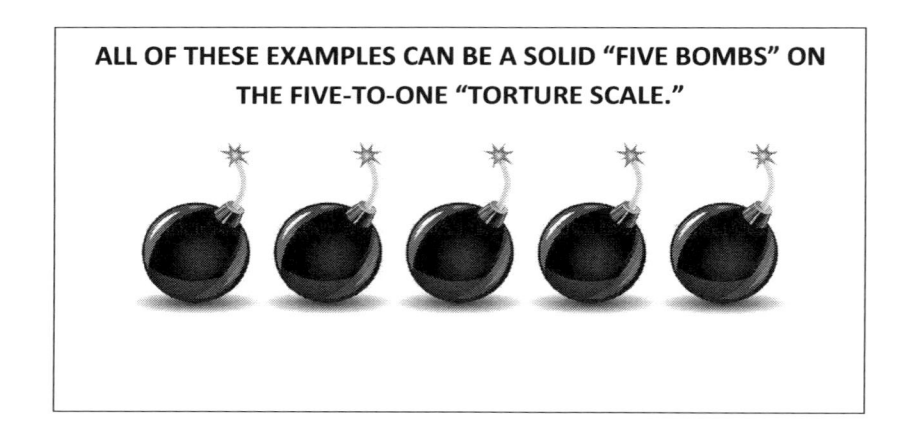

**ALL OF THESE EXAMPLES CAN BE A SOLID "FIVE BOMBS" ON THE FIVE-TO-ONE "TORTURE SCALE."**

© 2021 Charles J. Clarke III. "Bulls, Owls, Lambs and Tigers®" is a registered federal trademark of Charles J. Clarke III since 1988. Personality Selling™ and BOLT™ are Trademarks of Charles J. Clarke III. NO reproduction in any form is allowed.

# NOTES

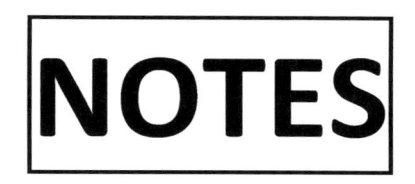

THINGS I AGREE WITH

THINGS I DISAGREE WITH

THINGS I NEED TO WORK ON

ACTION PLAN FOR ME

# Bulls, Owls, Lambs and Tigers®: Personality Selling™

## CHAPTER 38

## LIE/MYTH #35: SELLING IN A MARRIAGE IS VERY DIFFERENT THAN SELLING PRODUCT.

**SELLING IS SELLING!**

WE ARE GOING FROM SELLING IN A RESTAURANT TO SELLING IN A MARRIAGE, QUITE A SHIFT, YET A SIMILAR CONCEPT.

**EXAMPLE FROM MARRIAGE COUNSELING**

WHILE I WAS AN INSTRUCTOR AT TWO DIFFERENT UNIVERSITIES (UNIVERSITY OF MARYLAND AND UNIVERSITY OF ARIZONA), WHILE WORKING TOWARDS MY PH.D. IN SOCIOLOGY, I DID PART-TIME MARRIAGE COUNSELING AT BOTH UNIVERSITIES.

HERE IS AN EXAMPLE OF <u>SELLING</u> OR <u>NOT SELLING</u> IN A MARRIAGE.

**GIFT GIVING**

THIS COULD POSSIBLY BE ANOTHER MYTH.

IS IT BEST TO GIVE GIFTS TO YOUR SPOUSE OR A LOVED ONE THAT YOU PERSONALLY WOULD LIKE TO RECEIVE? ANSWER? IT DEPENDS!

IT DEPENDS ON <u>YOUR</u> PERSONALITY AND THEIRS. WHEN I WAS DEPARTMENT CHAIRMAN AND PROFESSOR AT MOUNT MERCY COLLEGE IN CEDAR RAPIDS, IOWA, I TAUGHT A COURSE CALLED "SOCIOLOGY OF FAMILY AND MARRIAGE," I EMPHASIZED HOW THE RESEARCH INDICATED THAT, "OPPOSITES ATTRACT." ARE YOU PERSONALLY INVOLVED IN A MARRIAGE OR SIGNIFICANT OTHER RELATIONSHIP WITH A "TOTAL OPPOSITE" OF YOUR PERSONALITY? IT APPEARS THAT OPPOSITES <u>DO</u> ATTRACT. MY LITTLE TWIST IS, "OPPOSITES ATTRACT AND GET MARRIED AND THEN SPEND THE REST OF THEIR LIFE TRYING TO GET OUT OF IT." YOUR THOUGHTS?

# Bulls, Owls, Lambs and Tigers®: Personality Selling™

> **"APPLE PEELER" STORY**

I WAS DOING MARRIAGE COUNSELING WITH A COUPLE WHO WERE QUITE OPPOSITE IN THEIR PERSONALITIES. SHE WAS A TIGER/TIGER AND HE WAS AN OWL/OWL. IT WAS THE SECOND MARRIAGE FOR EACH OF THEM. THEY WERE IN THEIR EARLY 40'S.

I HAD COUNSELED WITH THEM SEVERAL TIMES, AND THEY ALWAYS CAME IN TOGETHER. NEAR THE END, HE CAME IN BY HIMSELF AND SAID THAT <u>SHE</u> DID NOT WANT TO COME INTO COUNSELING ANYMORE, BUT HE SAID HE DID WANT TO CONTINUE, "BECAUSE DIVORCES WERE VERY EXPENSIVE." HE TOLD ME HE WANTED TO GIVE HER A "BIRTHDAY GIFT" AND ASKED IF I HAD ANY SUGGESTIONS FOR HER BIRTHDAY, A MONTH LATER.

I ASKED HIM IF HE HAD EVER GIVEN HER AN "I'M THINKING OF YOU PRESENT," RATHER THAN FOR AN OCCASION? HE REPLIED, "NO." HE SAID HE ALWAYS REMEMBERED HER BIRTHDAY, EVERY HOLIDAY AND ANNIVERSARY AND HE ALWAYS MADE SURE HIS SECRETARY PICKED OUT THE APPROPRIATE PRESENT. WE LEFT THAT SESSION, ON THAT NOTE.

A FEW DAYS LATER, WHEN HE HAD HIS NEXT APPOINTMENT, HE SAID HE HAD JUST GIVEN HER, THE NIGHT BEFORE, AN "I'M THINKING OF YOU" PRESENT. HE SAID IT "BACK-FIRED" ON HIM AND THAT SHE HAD PACKED UP AND LEFT HIM THE NIGHT BEFORE.

OF COURSE, AS ANY GOOD COUNSELOR WOULD DO, I WAS "STOIC" AND ASKED "WHAT DID YOU GIVE HER?"

NOW, HERE IS A MAN WHO DROVE A LARGE MERCEDES AND COULD HAVE AFFORDED MOST ANY KIND OF GIFT. HIS ANSWER WAS,

> **"I GAVE HER A BRAND-NEW APPLE PEELER."**

I REMAINED "STOIC" AND ASKED, "WHY?" HE SAID HE HAD GIVEN IT A LOT OF THOUGHT (AND HE HAD) AND HE REMEMBERED THAT THE LAST TIME SHE WAS PEELING APPLES WITH THE RUSTY, OLD APPLE PEELER (TO MAKE APPLE SAUCE), SHE HAD "BLOODIED" HER HAND.

HE WENT ON TO TELL ME THAT THEY HAD A "BACK 40" WITH AN APPLE ORCHARD AND SHE <u>CANNED</u> LARGE AMOUNTS OF APPLE SAUCE EVERY YEAR. I ASKED HIM WHO'S IDEA WAS THAT AND HIS ANSWER, OF COURSE, WAS IT WAS HIS IDEA, SO THEY WOULDN'T WASTE THE APPLES. IT TURNED OUT SHE DIDN'T LIKE DOING IT AND THOUGHT IT WAS A WASTE OF TIME AND WAS ONLY DOING IT OUT OF LOVE FOR HIM. HIS OWL THOUGHT IT WAS A "PRACTICAL" THING TO DO.

# Bulls, Owls, Lambs and Tigers®: Personality Selling™

I ASKED HIM IF HE WRAPPED THE "PRESENT" AND HE SAID, "YES," THAT HE HAD PUT IT IN A BOX THAT WAS ABOUT 2 INCHES WIDE AND 8 INCHES LONG. HE USED RECYCLED WRAPPING PAPER AND RECYCLED RIBBON AND BOW.

I ASKED ABOUT HER REACTION BEFORE SHE OPENED IT AND HE EXPLAINED HOW EXCITED SHE WAS. I FOUND OUT LATER SHE THOUGHT IT WAS JEWELRY (AND IT WASN'T).

I ASKED WHAT HER REACTION WAS WHEN SHE OPENED IT. HE SAID, "SHE THREW IT AT ME, STARTED SWEARING, WENT IN, PACKED A SUITCASE, AND SAID, "I'M OUT OF HERE," AND LEFT.

**WOW!**

HE WENT ON TO SAY, "I JUST DON'T UNDERSTAND HER."

THE TRUTH IS HE DIDN'T UNDERSTAND HER AND SHE DIDN'T UNDERSTAND HIM.

**POINT ABOUT SELLING**

SOMETIMES WE REALLY DON'T UNDERSTAND OUR "BUYERS," JUST LIKE THE MAN MENTIONED ABOVE DIDN'T UNDERSTAND HIS WIFE, AND SHE DIDN'T UNDERSTAND HIM.

**THEY WERE BOTH TORTURING EACH OTHER WITHOUT REALLY BEING AWARE OF IT.**

AN ANALOGY IS, "HE WAS SCRATCHING WHERE IT ITCHED FOR HIM, BUT NOT FOR HER."

DO YOU EVER DO THAT?

"SELLING IS SELLING," WHETHER IT IS SELLING IN A MARRIAGE OR SELLING PRODUCT TO A STRANGER.

WE NEED TO NEVER LOSE SIGHT OF THE NEEDS OF THE OTHER PERSON.

DO YOU SEE HOW THIS EXAMPLE FITS INTO THE ENTIRE ARENA OF LIES AND MYTHS WE HAVE BEEN TAUGHT IN SELLING™?

**Bulls, Owls, Lambs and Tigers®: Personality Selling™**

> ONE MORE POINT ABOUT GIFT GIVING

---

**BULLS AND OWLS THINK GIVING MONEY AS A GIFT IS "COOL." (WHO WOULDN'T WANT MONEY?)**

**LAMBS AND TIGERS THINK GIVING MONEY "STINKS," BECAUSE THEY DON'T FEEL ANY "THOUGHT" WENT INTO THE GIFT GIVING.**

**ASK AROUND. IT'S TRUE.**

---

DON'T "SELL" THE WAY YOU WANT TO BE SOLD.

SELL THE WAY THEY WANT TO BE SOLD.

GIVE WHAT THEY WANT, NOT WHAT YOU WANT.

ONE MORE THOUGHT IN THE AREA OF MARRIAGE.

HOW MANY OF YOU HAVE HAD VERBAL "FIGHTS" OVER "STUPID STUFF?"

ONE SPOUSE SAYS "REMEMBER THE TIME, ONE YEAR AGO, IN SAN DIEGO, WHEN WE WERE STAYING AT THE MARRIOTT? THE OTHER SPOUSE INTERRUPTS AND SAYS, "IT WAS THE HILTON." THE FIRST SPOUSE INSISTS IT WAS THE MARRIOTT AND THEY SPEND LOTS OF WAISTED TIME ARGUING ABOUT WHICH HOTEL IT WAS.

**BOTTOM LINE, "WHO CARES?"**

**QUIT ALWAYS HAVING TO BE "RIGHT!'**

YOUR THOUGHTS?

# Bulls, Owls, Lambs and Tigers®: Personality Selling™

THESE ARE ONLY A COUPLE EXAMPLES.

WE "TORTURE" OUR LOVED ONES, BECAUSE "WE HAVE TO BE RIGHT," AND EVEN GIVE THE GIFTS WE WOULD WANT, INSTEAD OF GIVING WHAT THEY WOULD WANT.

**THIS CAN BE A "FIVE BOMB" ON THE FIVE-TO-ONE "TORTURE SCALE," AND EVENTUALLY END IN DIVORCE.**

# NOTES

THINGS I AGREE WITH

THINGS I DISAGREE WITH

THINGS I NEED TO WORK ON

ACTION PLAN FOR ME

# CHAPTER 39

## LIE/MYTH #36: MASTER CLOSERS CAN NOT OVERCOME BAD OR FLAWED DESIGN

**BE CAREFUL WITH THIS ONE! NOT EVERYONE LIKES OR DISLIKES WHAT YOU LIKE OR DISLIKE.** WHAT <u>YOU</u> THINK IS BAD DESIGN OR FLAWED PRODUCT, SOMEONE ELSE MAY NOT THINK THE SAME WAY. THEY MAY LOVE IT!

EXAMPLE: IN PHOENIX, A COMMUNITY <u>HAD NOT HAD A SALE FOR 90 DAYS.</u> THE SALESLADY HAD "ISSUES" WITH THE MODEL, FLOOR PLANS, INVENTORY HOMES, LAYOUT OF THE COMMUNITY, AND THEIR PRICING. SHE HAD BEEN WITH THAT COMPANY FOR SEVERAL YEARS AND HAD RECENTLY BEEN TRANSFERRED TO THIS COMMUNITY WITH ZERO LOT LINES. SHE SAID THE COMMUNITY WAS BASICALLY <u>BAD PRODUCT</u> AND THE FLOOR PLANS WERE <u>FLAWED DESIGNS.</u>

I SUGGESTED WE TRANSFER HER FROM THE COMMUNITY AND HIRE A BRAND-NEW SALESPERSON FOR THAT COMMUNITY. WE HELD A "GROUP INTERVIEW" AND HIRED A MAN, NAMED JERRY M., WHO HAD NEVER PROFESSIONALY SOLD ANYTHING IN HIS LIFE. HE WAS IMMEDIATELY PUT THROUGH MY MASTER CLOSER TRILOGY, PLUS TWO ADDITIONAL DAYS OF ROLE PLAYING AND PDR (PRACTICE, DRILL AND REHEARSING).

**HERE'S THE BOTTOM LINE:**

IN HIS FIRST 30 DAYS OF SELLING, HE HAD 14 "GROSS" SALES AND 12 "NET" SALES: FULL PRICE, NO "GIVEAWAYS," NO CHANGE ORDERS AND 12 VERY HAPPY HOMEOWNERS.

**THIS CAN APPLY TO <u>EVERY</u> INDUSTRY.**

WHEN THE PREVIOUS SALESLADY WAS SELLING, THE OBJECTIONS WERE **HER OWN**. DON'T LET THAT INTERFERE WITH YOU. JERRY M. HAD NO PREVIOUS INTERNAL OBJECTIONS OR "MYTHS IN SELLING NEW HOMES™." HE FOLLOWED THE "MASTER CLOSER" PROGRAM.

**WHAT ABOUT YOU?**

THE TORTURE IS AGAIN ON THE COMPANY FOR <u>LOST SALES.</u>

# NOTES

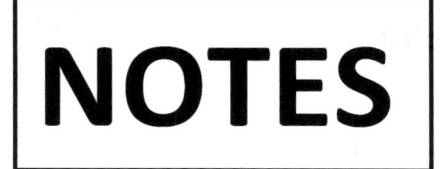

THINGS I AGREE WITH

THINGS I DISAGREE WITH

THINGS I NEED TO WORK ON

ACTION PLAN FOR ME

**Bulls, Owls, Lambs and Tigers®: Personality Selling™**

# CHAPTER 40

## CONCLUSION

THE BEST CONCLUSION FOR, "BULLS, OWLS, LAMBS & TIGERS®: PERSONALITY SELLING™" IS THE FOLLOWING CASE STUDY. THIS EXAMPLE INCORPORATES ALL 36 SALES PRINCIPLES IN THIS BOOK.

I HAVE TENS OF THOUSANDS OF EXAMPLES OF MASTER CLOSERS SIMILAR TO THIS FROM COAST TO COAST. THESE MASTER CLOSERS USING THESE PRINCIPLES ARE FROM EVERY PROFESSION (NO MATTER WHAT SIZE THE COMPANY).

THE FOLLOWING IS MY BEST EXAMPLE OF MY "MASTERPIECE AT WORK," WHERE AN ENTIRE SALES TEAM (EVENTHOUGH SMALL) USES ALL THESE PRINCIPLES ALL THE TIME. AGAIN, ALL ARE MASTER CLOSERS ALWAYS USING ALL THE PRINCIPLES AND GETTING STAGERING RESULTS (100%+ INCREASE IN A VERY SHORT PERIOD OF TIME.)

I WAS THE DIRECTOR OF SALES FROM LATE 2017 THROUGH APRIL 2021 AT BROWN HAVEN HOMES. DURING THIS TIME PERIOD I ALSO CONTINUED MY OTHER CONSULTING AND SEMINARS.

---

MARCH 2021

**"RECORD-SHATTERING" NEW HOME CONSULTANT SELLS "91" NEW CUSTOM HOMES IN HIAWASSEE, GEORGIA IN 2020** BY CHARLES J. CLARKE III, DIRECTOR OF SALES, BROWN HAVEN HOMES.

Subrina Abernathy, New Home Consultant, in Hiawassee, Georgia, with Brown Haven Homes, (www.brownhavenhomes.com) sold "91" Brand New, "On-Your-Lot" Custom Homes in 2020 (not all closed in 2020).

**In 2020 she had an "Unbelievable-but-True," 1 in 3 closing ratio with over ½ of her sales closed the very first day of contact, with a signed contract and deposit.**

That is a record, since the closing ratio of all companies, nationally, is approximately a 1 in 15, with it being "very rare" to sell a prospect the very first day.

Congratulations to Subrina Abernathy, "The #1 New Home Sales Specialist in the Nation!" (That is a quote from Subrina, but it is true!

SUBRINA'S GOAL FOR 2020 WAS 100 SALES BUT THE CORONOVIRUS SLOWED HER BUYERS DOWN IN THE EARLY MONTHS TO "ONLY" 5 SALES PER MONTH. SHE FIGURED OUT THE POWER OF "VIRTUAL PRESENTATIONS," (SHE PREFERS IN-PERSON PRESENTATIONS). SHE WAS STILL ABLE TO INCLUDE ALL

# Bulls, Owls, Lambs and Tigers®: Personality Selling™

THE STEPS SHE DOES IN PERSON, ON THE FIRST DAY. THAT INCLUDES QUALIFYING FOR THE BUYER'S TIME FRAME (READY), CHOICE OF PLAN (WILLING), AND THEIR FINANCIAL ABILITY (ABLE). SHE THEN DOES A, "FULL-BLOWN COMPUTERIZED PRICE QUOTE," (PRESENTATION). SHE THEN ASKS THEM, "HOW DO YOU LIKE EVERYTHING YOU HAVE SEEN TODAY?" "HOW DO YOU LIKE THIS HOME?" "WHAT DO YOU THINK ABOUT GOING AHEAD WITH THIS TODAY?" SHE DOES THIS 100% OF THE TIME. MOST SALESPEOPLE DO <u>NOT</u> DO ALL THAT THE FIRST DAY BECAUSE THEY HOLD ONTO THE MYTH THAT PEOPLE DO NOT BUY A NEW HOME THE FIRST DAY. "YES! THEY DO IF THEY ARE ASKED!"

SUBRINA SAYS, "IT IS ALL ABOUT 'CUSTOMER SERVICE' AND SATISFYING ALL THE BUYERS' TRUE NEEDS; EMOTIONALLY AND PERSONALLY." SHE IS VERY PATIENT AND "THOROUGH" THE VERY FIRST DAY, WHICH ACCOUNTS FOR 50% OF HER 91 SALES DONE THE FIRST DAY. (HALF WOULD "NEVER" BUY THE FIRST DAY AND THAT IS CERTAINLY OKAY WITH HER. THEY BUY THE SECOND DAY.)

SHE GOES ON TO SAY, "BROWN HAVEN HOMES IS THE MOST AMAZING COMPANY FOR WHOM ANYONE COULD WORK, OR FROM WHOM TO BUY A HOME." BEFORE COMING TO BROWN HAVEN HOMES NEARLY THREE YEARS AGO SHE HAD BEEN A BARTENDER AND HAD NEVER BEEN INVOLVED WITH ANY FORM OF HOME SALES.

AGAIN, BROWN HAVEN HOMES IS AN "ON-YOUR-LOT BUILDER," WHICH MEANS BROWN HAVEN HOMES BUILDS ON THE BUYER'S LAND OR LAND THAT BROWN HAVEN HOMES HELPS THE BUYER OBTAIN. APPROXIMATELY ½ OF HER SALES ARE DONE WITH BUYERS THAT DO NOT HAVE LAND.

THE HOME OFFICE OF BROWN HAVEN HOMES IS IN BLAIRSVILLE, GEORGIA WITH SALES LOCATIONS IN HIAWASSEE, GEORGIA; ELLIJAY, GEORGIA; DAWSONVILLE, GEORGIA (ATLANTA AREA); ASHEVILLE, NORTH CAROLINA; ANDERSON, SOUTH CAROLINA; AND CHATTANOOGA, TENNESSEE. EACH OF THE LOCATIONS **HAS A WORLD-CLASS DESIGN STUDIO** FOR "ONE-STOP SHOPPING." BROWN HAVEN HOMES DOES NOT HAVE "TRADITIONALLY-FURNISHED MODEL HOMES," BUT DOES HAVE OTHER PROGRAMS.

THERE ARE A TOTAL OF 7 "MASTER CLOSERS" (NEW HOME CONSULTANTS) AT THE 6 LOCATIONS AND ALL THE OTHER 6 USE THE SAME SALES METHODOLOGIES AS SUBRINA AND ALL HAVE AT LEAST A 1 IN 5 CLOSING RATIOS. ("THE ABSOLUTE BEST 7-PERSON SALES TEAM IN THE NATION IN TERMS OF PERFORMANCE AND RESULTS!")

IN FEBRUARY THERE WERE FOUR SALESPEOPLE WHO HAD 11 TO 13 SALES IN THAT ONE MONTH. YES, SABRINA WAS ONE OF THEM.

SUBRINA ATTRIBUTES HER SUCCESS TO:

1) BROWN HAVEN HOMES' INCREDIBLE LEADERSHIP (JOHN ALLEN, PRESIDENT AND OWNER), LOCAL LEADERSHIP (RICHARD SMITH, GENERAL MANAGER), AND HER ENTIRE PROFESSIONAL LOCAL TEAM IN HIAWASSEE AND THEIR ABILITY TO BUILD THE MOST BEAUTIFUL AND FINEST QUALITY HOMES POSSIBLE, WITH SO MUCH ATTENTION TO DETAIL,

# Bulls, Owls, Lambs and Tigers®: Personality Selling™

2) HER AMAZING BUYERS WHO WANT ONLY THE BEST,

3) THE SELLING METHODOLOGIES OF CHARLES CLARKE III, DIRECTOR OF SALES OF BROWN HAVEN HOMES. HE ADVOCATES A 1 IN 3 CLOSING RATIO AND SAYS 50% OF ALL SALES **COULD** AND **SHOULD** BE DONE THE FIRST DAY. THAT IS WHAT SUBRINA AND THE OTHER 6 SALESPEOPLE AT BROWN HAVEN HOMES ACHIEVED IN 2020 AND WHAT THEY CONTINUE TO ACHIEVE IN 2021,

*WHEN CHARLES FIRST DID A TWO-DAY SEMINAR IN MAY 2017 FOR BROWN HAVEN HOMES, THEY WERE SELLING APPROXIMATELY 30 HOMES PER YEAR (2 TO 3 A MONTH) AND HAD A CLOSING RATIO OF APPROXIMATELY 1 IN 20. THIS CLOSING RATIO REFLECTS NO SALES HAVING BEEN DONE THE FIRST DAY.*

IN APRIL 2021, THE ENTIRE TEAM OF SIX LOCATIONS AND SIX SALESPEOPLE SOLD 61 SALES (NOT ALL CLOSED) WITH FOUR OF THE SIX NEW HOME CONSULTANTS SELLING **OVER** 10 EACH. YES, SUBRINA WAS ONE OF THEM.

CURRENT DAY, ALL 7 MASTER CLOSERS OF BROWN HAVEN HOMES, "TAKE ON THE PERSONALITY OF THEIR BUYERS," (**BOLT™**) THEY BECOME THE OTHER PERSON WHICH IS THE HIGHEST FORM OF "RESPECTING" THE OTHER PERSON. THEY ALL USE <u>ALL</u> THE 36 SALES PRINCIPLES FROM THIS BOOK.

THEY ARE ALL SO SPECIAL THEY DESERVE RECOGNITION: **SUBRINA ABERNATHY, HIAWASSEE, GEORGIA; KELSIE WARE BELL, ELLIJAY, GEORGIA; DUSTIN BURCH, DAWSONVILLE, GEORGIA (ATLANTA AREA); MICHAEL DAVIS, ASHEVILLE, NORTH CAROLINA; TREY HARIS, CHATTANOOGA, TENNESSEE; ETHAN BURCH, CHATTANOOGA, TENNESSEE, AND TOM VALICHKA, ROVING SALES MANAGER.** IF YOU ARE IN THEIR AREA STOP BY AND SAY, "HELLO!" AND **BUY A HOME!**

ALL 7 OF THESE NEW HOME CONSULTANTS ARE IN THEIR MID-TWENTIES OR THIRTIES WITH **ZERO** PRIOR EXPERIENCE IN SELLING HOMES (NEW OR EXISTING). THEY WERE ALL, "CLEAN SLATES," WITH NO PRIOR RIGHT-OR-WRONG WAY OF SELLING HOMES.

ISN'T THIS A FANTASTIC EXAMPLE OF PUTTING ALL THIS INTO PRACTICE? THERE ARE HUNDREDS OF THOUSANDS OF EXAMPLES OF MY MASTER CLOSERS USING THESE EXACT SUGGESTIONS AND METHODOLOGIES. THE PREVIOUS EXAMPLE IS ONLY ONE EXAMPLE BUT ONE THE <u>BEST</u> EXAMPLES OF THE ENTIRE TEAM BEING MASTER CLOSERS.

# NOTES

THINGS I AGREE WITH

THINGS I DISAGREE WITH

THINGS I NEED TO WORK ON

ACTION PLAN FOR ME

# Bulls, Owls, Lambs and Tigers®: Personality Selling™

## CHAPTER 41

### FINAL THOUGHTS

THESE 36 LIES AND MYTHS IN SELLING ARE ONLY THE "TIP OF THE ICEBURG." YOU CAN SEE THAT ALOT OF THE CHAPTERS HAVE "SUB" LIES AND MYTHS.

I INVITE YOU TO SEND ME OTHER "LIES AND MYTHS" IN SELLING THAT YOU COME ACROSS, SO I CAN INCLUDE THEM IN VOLUME II, ALONG WITH YOUR NAME AND COMPANY.

> **WE, IN SELLING, HAVE BEEN "TAUGHT" THE FINE ART OF "TORTURING" OUR BUYERS THROUGH THESE "LIES AND MYTHS." LET'S NOT CONTINUE THESE METHODS.**

THESE ARE JUST THIRTY-SIX EXAMPLES. WE SOMETIMES DO IT **INNOCENTLY,** OR SOMETIMES VERY OBTRUSIVELY. OFTEN, WE ARE JUST "SELLING THE WAY WE WOULD LIKE TO BE SOLD," OR APPLYING WHAT HAS BEEN TAUGHT TO US, THROUGH THESE LIES AND MYTHS. EITHER WAY, WE CERTAINLY END UP "TORTURING" MANY OF OUR BUYERS.

WE TORTURE THEM BY: NOT GIVING THEM THE PRICE WHEN THEY WANT IT, TRYING TO CONTROL THE SALE, WANTING TO BE THEIR FRIEND AND TALK ABOUT SOCIAL FIRST WHEN ALL THEY WANT TO DO IS "BUY IT," NOT LET THEM THINK IT ALL OVER IF THAT'S WHAT THEY WANT TO DO. WE TORTURE THEM WITH ALL THE REST OF THE LIES AND MYTHS IN THIS BOOK, AND MORE.

SOME ARE MAJOR "TORTURE SYSTEMS." SOME ARE MINOR "TORTURE SYSTEMS," YET IT IS STILL A FORM OF "SALES TORTURE."

GO THROUGH THE ENTIRE BOOK AGAIN.

WHICH WERE YOUR FAVORITE CHAPTERS? WHY?

WHICH WERE YOUR LEAST FAVORITE CHAPTERS? WHY?

ALL OF THE CHAPTERS "FIT" TOGETHER, EVEN THE ONES THAT DON'T APPLY TO YOUR OWN INDIVIDUAL INDUSTRY. THERE ARE "ASPECTS" FROM EVERY CHAPTER THAT WILL MAKE YOU A STRONGER SALESPERSON AND A MASTER CLOSER, GAINING THE RESPECT FROM YOUR CUSTOMERS AND THUS MAKING YOU AND YOUR COMPANY MORE MONEY AND A STRONGER COMPANY.

© 2021 Charles J. Clarke III. "Bulls, Owls, Lambs and Tigers®" is a registered federal trademark of Charles J. Clarke III since 1988. Personality Selling™ and BOLT™ are Trademarks of Charles J. Clarke III. NO reproduction in any form is allowed.

# Bulls, Owls, Lambs and Tigers®: Personality Selling™

BUYERS ALL AROUND THE NATION, AND IN OTHER COUNTRIES, ARE SAYING, "JUST SELL ME THE WAY I WANT TO BE SOLD, NOT HOW YOU WANT TO SELL ME." "GIVE ME WHAT I WANT, WHEN I WANT IT." "I HAVE BEEN 'TORTURED' BY SALESPEOPLE LONG ENOUGH."

WHAT ARE YOUR THOUGHTS?

> HAS THIS BOOK HELPED YOU TO THINK DIFFERENTLY ABOUT THE SALES PROCESS, AS PROMISED?

AGAIN, THIS IS A TYPE OF BOOK THAT YOU REALLY NEED TO READ SEVERAL TIMES MORE. DO YOU THINK ANY DIFFERENTLY ABOUT THE SALES PROCESS, THEN YOU DID BEFORE READING THIS?

> WOULD YOU AGREE THAT THIS IS NOT AN "ORDINARY" BOOK?

GO BACK AND LOOK AT THE "36 LIES AND MYTHS" AGAIN. HAS YOUR OPINION CHANGED? HOW MANY YES'S DO YOU NOW HAVE?

MAKE A LIST OF THINGS YOU ARE GOING TO BE DOING DIFFERENTLY.

KEEP IN TOUCH!

CHARLES J. CLARKE III

EMAIL = CHARLES@PERSONALITYSELLING.COM

WEBSITE = WWW.PERSONALITYSELLING.COM

---

**IF YOU REALLY LIKED THIS BOOK, ORDER A COPY FOR EVERYONE IN YOUR COMPANY. MAKE THESE PRINCIPLES A WAY OF LIFE IN YOUR COMPANY.**

---

© 2021 Charles J. Clarke III. "Bulls, Owls, Lambs and Tigers®" is a registered federal trademark of Charles J. Clarke III since 1988. Personality Selling™ and BOLT™ are Trademarks of Charles J. Clarke III. NO reproduction in any form is allowed.

## About The Author

Charles J. Clarke III is the Inventor, Creator and Founder of, "Bulls, Owls, Lambs and Tigers®." He is, "The Authority" on Temperament, Personality, and Personality Selling™.

Charles is a Behavioral Scientist (Sociologist) and was a former College Professor and Department Chairman of Sociology. He has conducted scientific research with over 300,000 participants and continues to do research on, "Bulls, Owls, Lambs and Tigers®."

Through the last 33 years Charles has been lecturing, doing seminars and consulting on his topic of, "Bulls, Owls, Lambs and Tigers®, BOLT™ (which is an acronym) and Personality Selling™. He has conducted over 3,500 lectures and seminars to over ½ million+ attendees in forty-nine states in America and other countries (Canada, Mexico, Hungary, and England).

He has been on television, radio and has been written up in magazines and newspapers from coast-to-coast. Charles has written, "mini books" but not until now has his, "two, full-volume books" on, "Bulls, Owls, Lambs and Tigers®" and "Bulls, Owls, Lambs and Tigers®: Personality Selling™" been published.

"Bulls, Owls, Lambs and Tigers®" is a Registered Federal Trademark of Charles J. Clarke III, as well as BOLT™ and Personality Selling™ being trademarks of Charles J. Clarke III. All his "Bulls, Owls, Lambs and Tigers®," BOLT™, and Personality Selling™ is his copywritten material.

Enjoy the ride!

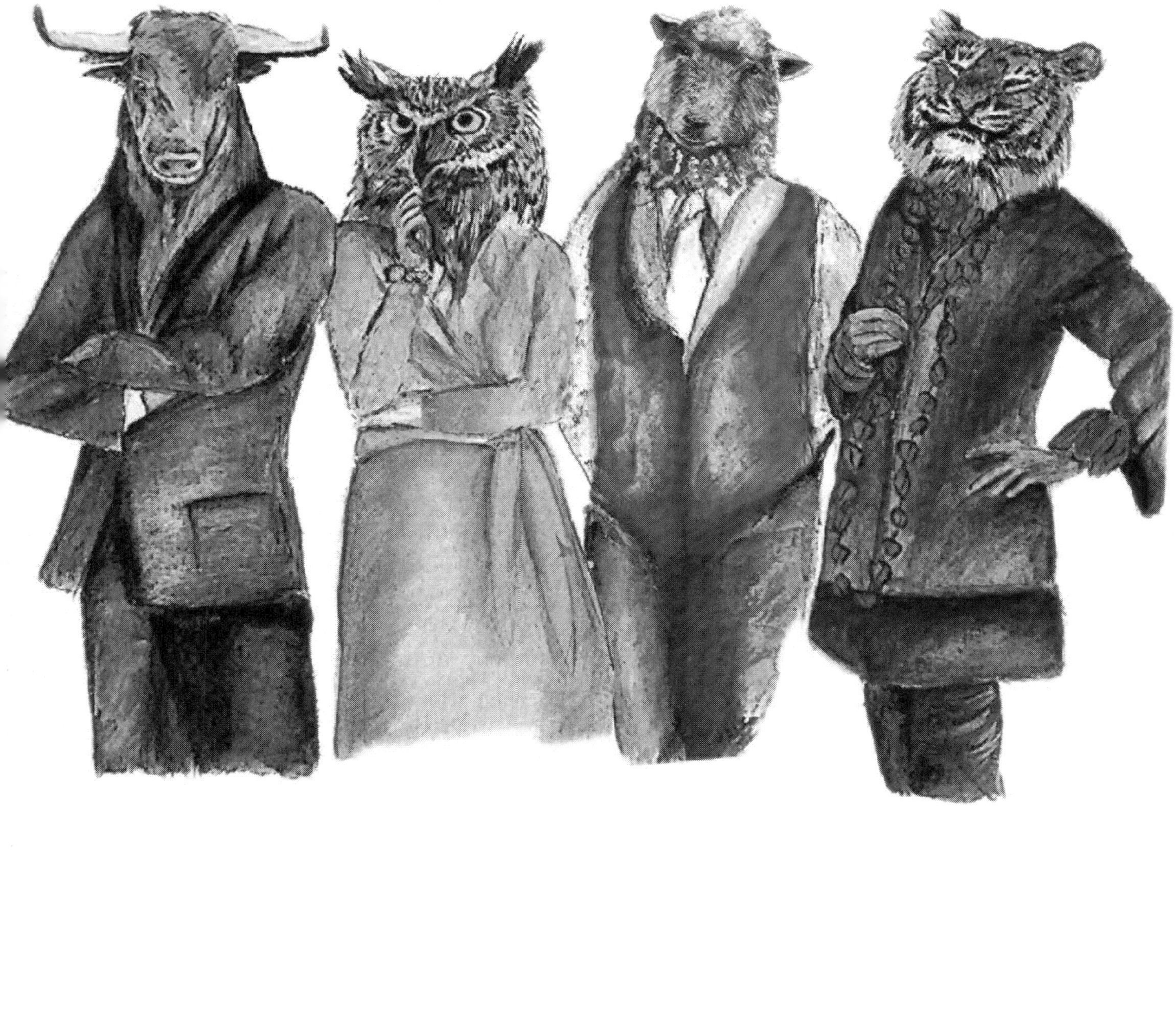

# BULLS, OWLS, LAMBS AND TIGERS®: PERSONALITY SELLING™

## OWL

- Urgency Closes *do not* work with Owls
- Value Closes *work best* with Owls
- T-Bar Closes *work well* with Owls
- Ben Franklin Closes *work well* with Owls
- Flip Chart Presentations *work well* with the Owl

**The Owl** is not pushy and not very emotional
**The Owl** is extremely analytical and detailed oriented
**The Owl's** driving force is…

### Order

*Be the Owl with the Owl*

## BULL

- Urgency Closes Motivate Bulls
- Take Away Closes Motivate Bulls
- Bulls *do not like* questions answered with questions
- Bulls *take less* time to buy
- If you negotiate the price with a Bull they *WILL NOT* buy from you that day. They will think they can get it lower the next time
- Bulls *love to bluff*
- Convince the Bull that you *do not* lower the price

**The Bull** is highly pushy and not very emotional, except for anger
**The Bull** is a business first person who like the bottom line and likes people to get to the point
**The Bull's** driving force is ….

### Control

*Be the Bull with the Bull*

## LAMB

- Urgency Closes *do not* work with Lambs (they make Lambs not want to come back)
- Be their friend
- Imagination Closes
- "I Feel Your Pain" Close (Feel, Felt, Found)
- "You Deserve It" Close
- *TELL* them to buy
- Think it Over Close

**The Lamb** is not pushy but very emotional
**The Lamb** is very kind and does not like conflict
**The Lamb's** driving force is…

### Pleasing Others

*Be the Lamb with the Lamb*

## TIGER

- Urgency Closes *motivate* Tigers
- Take Away Closes *motivate* Tigers
- Tigers will buy the very first time in (even the *MOST* expensive properties)
- If a Tiger *is not closed on the first visit* the probability is extremely high that you will never see them again
- Negotiating Closes

**The Tiger** is highly pushy and highly emotional
**The Tiger** usually does not want all of the details
**The Tiger's** driving force is…

### Fun and Excitement

*Be the Tiger with the Tiger*

© 2021 Charles J. Clarke III. "Bulls, Owls, Lambs and Tigers®" is a registered federal trademark of Charles J. Clarke III since 1988. Personality Selling™ and BOLT™ are Trademarks of Charles J. Clarke III. NO reproduction in any form is allowed.

Made in the USA
Las Vegas, NV
21 September 2021